Praise for *The Journey of Not Knowing*

"The Journey of Not Knowing beautifully breaks the business book mold and should be required reading for leaders...[It] uses a cleverly constructed parable to demonstrate how to navigate business uncertainty. In modern business, one of the most significant challenges leaders face is moving an organization forward even when the answers to critical questions may be unknown. Coping with "not knowing" is the theme of Julie Benezet's expertly written book."

—Foreword Clarion Reviews

"Benezet offers a management handbook geared toward the unconventional in the modern business world . . . [She] makes crystalline sense; for example, she writes relatively early on that it's more important than ever for managers to know themselves—to know . . ."who you are and for what you stand" in a world of shifting expectations and constantly looming unknowns.

—Kirkus Reviews

". . .This book contains many jewels on how one deals with making decisions based on uncertain information. Despite the ubiquitous reliance on data collection and analysis, many business decisions are still based on a form of intuition. In most cases, the most important thing is to have the courage to act on those beliefs rather than playing it safe and eventually sorry."

—Charles Ashbacher, Charles Ashbacher Reviews,
Top 50 Amazon Reviewer

". . . The Journey of Not Knowing provides a great teaching tool for both established and emerging leaders. The book skillfully raises awareness of how defensive behaviors against the unknown can get in the way of their success as leaders, and how they might overcome them to achieve strategic results. . . I highly recommend this great read."

—Patricia Langer, EVP, Human Resources
at NBC Universal, Inc.

"The Journey of Not Knowing combines the many years of business world experience of its author with astute observation of human behavior. . . Benezet intimately describes the evolution of a leadership team from resistance to engagement in order to solve a critical business problem. The Journey model included at the back of the book explains how they got there. The book is fresh, fun and inspiring."

—Cindy Aden, Librarian, Former Amazonian
and current Washington State Librarian

JULIE BENEZET

About the Author

JULIE BENEZET has devoted her professional life to exploring the new, building businesses and helping others do the same. She currently works as a leadership consultant, teacher, and owner of The Journey of Not Knowing, a leadership program she founded. She speaks and writes on leading and living in the 21st Century and decoding human behavior in the face of change.

Julie spent four years as a member of the Amazon.com leadership team that brought the company from the early steep ramp up phase to its emergence as a thriving enterprise. Before joining Amazon.com, Julie built businesses and raised capital for a broad range of industries from Fortune 100 companies to start-ups. She practiced law in New York and Seattle.

Julie loves both to learn and teach. She led the "Challenges of Leadership" program for executives at the Harvard Graduate School of Design for ten years. She has appeared in numerous publications including *The Wall Street Journal*, *The New York Times*, *Tech Republic.com*, *Training Industry* and *The Zweig Letter*. She holds an LLB (law) and M.Sc. (psychology) from McGill University and a B.A. from Cornell University.

When she is not working, she loves to read mysteries, explore new wineries, and wander through compelling physical environments.

For more information, visit.
www.juliebenezet.com

You can subscribe to her blog, "The View from the Treehouse," at www.juliebenezet.com/blog

THE JOURNEY OF NOT KNOWING

THE
JOURNEY
OF NOT
KNOWING

HOW 21ST CENTURY LEADERS
CAN CHART A COURSE
WHERE THERE IS NONE

A Story

JULIE BENEZET

MORTON HILL PRESS
Ashland, Oregon

The Journey of Not Knowing
How 21st-Century Leaders Can Chart a Course Where There Is None

Published by Morton Hill Press
PO Box 614
Ashland, Oregon 97520
www.journeyofnotknowing.com

ISBN: 978-0-9978139-0-6

Library of Congress Control Number: 2016912056

Publisher's Cataloging-In-Publication Data
(Prepared by The Donohue Group, Inc.)

Names: Benezet, Julie.
Title: The journey of not knowing : how 21st century leaders can chart a course where there is none : a story / Julie Benezet.
Description: [Ashland, Oregon] : [Morton Hill Press], [2016]
Identifiers: LCCN 2016912056 | ISBN 978-0-9978139-0-6 |
  ISBN 978-0-9978139-1-3 (ebook)
Subjects: LCSH: Leadership. | Uncertainty. | Success in business.
Classification: LCC HD57.7 .B46 2016 (print) | LCC HD57.7 (ebook) | DDC 658.4092–dc23

Content editor: Gail M. Kearns, www.topressandbeyond.com
Copyeditor: Joni Wilson
Book and cover design: theBookDesigners
Book production coordinated by To Press & Beyond
Book cover and layout images © Shutterstock

DISCLAIMER

To my family, for all its love and support,
and to my brother, in memory of all those tree houses.

CONTENTS

INTRODUCTION

I SPENT THE first half of my youth in a treehouse, or at least that is where my mind lived. While the neighborhood children rode bicycles, played board games, and paged through story-books, I perched in my treehouse thinking about how I could make it better.

I'd look up into the upper branches of that big maple tree and wonder which of them could hold another seat, one high among the leaves that could be reached by an interesting progression of winding wooden slats, or one that would allow me to see farther across the neighborhood. You never knew who or what was out there, or how it would feel to be tucked up among the leaves with a lot of sky overhead and human activity below. That is, until you put those ideas into motion. Every year I figured out a new design. Then my brother set to work building it.

I don't wish to suggest I never rode bicycles, played board games, or read books. While I enjoyed those activities, my mind was forever pulled by the dreams of how could I create an environment that was more satisfying, useful, or compelling. I was a rather shy kid, and I noticed most of my friends found their bicycles and board games more interesting than my ideas. That made me nervous. Yet I continued to dream. Dreams fed me. Even better was actualizing them.

Cut to a few decades later. It was just after lunch. My blood sugar had peaked and was spiraling downward into a midafternoon lull. I sat in a small, sunny office opposite the CEO of a large, well-known company. We were exchanging random thoughts and anecdotes as we waited for the rest of the meeting attendees to assemble. At one point, we talked about what it was like to have a moment of stability when at least some of the trains were running on time.

It felt good to get to a place where not all actions required a major negotiation due to lack of procedures. Then we stopped, both of us sounding a little bored. The CEO said, "Every time I feel things starting to get calm, I have to turn them on their edge."

I chuckled. "Yes, and every time you do that, my life becomes insane." He let out one of his signature volcanic laughs.

I spent four years navigating Jeff Bezos' constant shifts in direction as we experimented with the new global business model called ecommerce. Our post-lunch conversation took place in 2001. I had been at Amazon for three years as its first global real estate executive. My job was to capture the company strategy and convert it into bricks and mortar, no easy matter when the company strategy traveled at the speed of bits and bytes and real estate travels at the speed of bricks.

The asynchronicity of the two worlds posed major challenges. At the same time, I thrived on it. The comment Bezos made to me resonated deeply. There was something familiar about the unease that comes with trying a new idea and then embarking on the adventure to see it through.

Finding and Avoiding Our Leadership Edge

During thirty-five years of business life, I have met many people like me. They showed up in every industry, geography, and size of organization. What we shared was a hunger to raise the game, take chances, and move things into a better future for our organizations. Our yearning often landed us in leadership roles, taking us through many unmarked pathways. We had an idea of where we wanted to end up, but until we got there, the outcome was unknown. Not knowing was scary, and scary was okay.

What we also shared, along the way, was how we inevitably tripped over our own blind spots and landed in box canyons we pretended weren't there. In reality, they were places to escape from the discomfort of not knowing whether our dreams would turn out. Eventually, with the help of intervening events, conversations, or moments of self-reflection, our hunger to see a new idea come to fruition took over. It allowed us to push past our discomfort to make our dreams come true, or find new ones that worked better.

The Journey of Not Knowing Book

This book explores the deep influence of the unknown on leadership and its critical importance to leadership success. It is organized into five parts.

PART 1: What Amazon Taught Me about Leadership and the Unknown. The genesis of this book came from my experiences and those of many others who have taken on leadership roles. The book opens with a personal story from my life at Amazon, and how the experiences there crystallized for me the fundamental linkage between leadership and the unknown. What we don't know, whether it is something about the environment in which we work or something that resides inside of us, can either drive us or get in the way.

PART 2: Leadership and the Unknown. While the unknown has always been relevant to leaders, the twenty-first century has upped the ante, as no one knows what is coming next. It is hard to hold all that anxiety. Many leaders deal with it by simply avoiding what they don't know. By doing so, they miss the opportunities in what they don't know but could find out to the benefit of their organizations and themselves. Part 2 describes the relevance of the unknown to leadership and a brief description of the Journey of Not Knowing principles.

PART 3: Arrow, Inc.: One Day in March. The Arrow, Inc., story comprises the bulk of the book. The narrative describes one business day in the lives of the leadership team at Arrow, Inc. While Arrow is a fictional company, its characters will be familiar to anyone who has worked with executive teams. During that day, to win a project with Porter, a new client critical to its business, the Arrow leadership team has to explain why a former client fired them.

None of the eight members of the Arrow leadership team knows the answer. In fact, until Porter asked its question, each has managed to avoid figuring out what happened. The Porter request forces the team to push through defensive and highly ineffective behaviors to solve the mystery of what they did not know about the former client. They also have to learn how their individual behaviors prevented them from unearthing the answer earlier.

PART 4: The Journey of Not Knowing Model. To start you on your own Journey of Not Knowing to more successful leadership, I have included a roadmap of the Journey of Not Knowing principles and examples from the Arrow story as to how they apply to its characters.

The roadmap represents the foundation of the Journey of Not Knowing leadership development program (http://www.journeyofnotknowing.com/). During the past six years, hundreds of executives from around the globe have participated in the program. They come from a wide diversity of large, medium, and small companies, including Microsoft, Mead Johnson, Philips, and King/Z2. The many participants with whom Journey program leaders have had the honor of working have further informed its principles and their application to the organizational world.

PART 5: The Reward of Taking the Journey: One Night at Amazon in Late December 1999. The final part of this book explains the value of taking the Journey and concludes with a second personal story from my Amazon days that took place on

December 23, 1999. It describes what I uncovered as an important personal guiding principle that not only got me through that year at Amazon, but also laid the foundation for the Journey of Not Knowing.

As will be revealed, the Arrow story illustrates that uncovering the truth about an organization and oneself releases the great potential that comes from confronting the unknown. It also demonstrates the loss of opportunity when ignored. That evolution is the Journey of Not Knowing.

Part 1

WHAT AMAZON TAUGHT ME ABOUT
LEADERSHIP AND THE UNKNOWN

Navigating the New

I JOINED AMAZON because it looked like a great adventure. At the time, I did not know how much of one it would be. I also did not foresee how it would fundamentally alter my view of leadership.

Amazon intrigued me with its energy, audacity, and willingness to plunge into places where others had not ventured. The people who worked there moved through the blur of a vast, unrelenting world of unknowns on a learning curve that pointed straight up.

As an executive, how I could best navigate this constantly changing environment came to me late one evening in January 1999. I did not grasp its full significance for leadership, however, until after the hunt for a large distribution center in Germany.

Early Amazon: A Few Liner Notes

What happened in Germany can be more easily understood when placed on a map of where Amazon was at the time.

Amazon brought together a group of smart, highly competitive, and entrepreneurial Gen Xers, along with a handful of Baby Boomers such as me. All of us shared a burning desire to prove we had a winning business model in the new world of ecommerce.

In those early days, outsiders viewed Amazon as an extraordinary case of organizational and strategic chaos that seemed to succeed despite itself. In fact, its mid-1990s push into the 24/7, hyper-connected, global world of work portended the future for the entire business world. Twenty years after Amazon opened its cyber doors, business everywhere has evolved to a state where chaos is the norm, and confronting it is both creative and essential.

I started my Amazon tenure during its young adolescent days. I reported to various "C's" in the C-suite and spent four amazing, mind-bending (not to mention aging) years there.

When I stepped into the shabby halls of Amazon on July 30, 1998, thirty other new recruits entered the building with me. At least another thirty persons arrived weekly at the Seattle head-quarters that year to participate in this great experiment. Many of them had previous corporate work experience. Others merely had an impressive grade point average from the college they had recently left. All had driven personalities. The organization chart, such as it was, lived on twenty-eight(ish) pages kept discretely in the Finance Department, who protected its constantly changing state from other eyes.

Outside the company, the world was becoming 24/7, digital, and fast. Amazon rode at the vanguard of that trend.

In 1998, Amazon offered more than four million book and music titles on the Internet to individual customers in more than 160 countries, an unprecedented feat. Before Amazon, consumers bought goods either in physical stores, filled with inventory shipped there in bulk, or from catalogs offering up to 5,000 products that could be shipped to their homes or businesses individually. The Internet had the potential to give individual consumers the ability to buy as many goods as existed in physical stores combined with the convenience of home delivery. In 1995, Amazon launched its business with the goal of taking on that bold bet.

The Internet as a product distribution channel spawned a new world of individual consumer reach, expectations, and power. Our job at Amazon was to invent a business to attract and retain customers whose demands evolved as we did.

Everything about Amazon resided in the unknown. Ecommerce was a new word. We worked in a new company with new technology, new global footprint, new people, and new breed of relationship with individual consumers. There also was the small matter of a new organization with a highly independent, overachieving workforce with a disdain for rules in any form.

Wall Street analysts both loved and hated Amazon's stock price. They looked for every opportunity to endorse and at the same time challenge its underpinnings. Inside the company, we focused on how to build a new business that would last for the long term, regardless of the near-term stock price. To do that, we had to address endless fundamental questions:

- Would individual consumers become comfortable with submitting their private credit card information to the Internet?

- What difference did pricing make in the online channel when weighed against the convenience of home-based ordering and delivery?

- Where on a website page would potential customers direct their attention, and what motivated them to buy something or leave the site?

- Would the hassle factor of returning a product without a bricks-and-mortar store to visit be a barrier to buying online?

- Would frank feedback from customers on products prevent product providers from playing?

- How smart would our fulfillment system have to be, and could others do it for us or would we have to do it all ourselves?

- Could we even create a global reach of individual customers who would eschew a visit to their local stores where they could touch and feel consumer goods in favor of deciding to buy something based on a photograph on their computer screens?

We had no idea how any of this would go. At best, what we had in front of us was a lot of trial and error. From my perch of figuring out how to deliver large chunks of real estate and other essential infrastructure to Amazon workers worldwide, I had to operate in the middle of the company's thrash through a sea of forever-changing information. To justify long-term investment of hundreds of millions of dollars in real estate, we had to develop credible underlying business-growth strategies without the benefit of existing business plans or even the mechanisms to develop them.

To say it was stressful would be an understatement. It was also exciting.

It Started in Fernley

On a dank, drippy Seattle night in January 1999, I sat alone in my interior, ill-lit Amazon office. It had been a particularly long day, and I needed a few minutes to reconstitute my brain before going home. As head of global real estate for Amazon, I surrounded myself with office trappings that were not only humble, but also demonstrated the thematic importance of frugality at Amazon—that is, thou shalt not spend a penny on anything that does not serve the customer directly.

Translated into office furniture, that meant a $129 plastic chair with a lurid green cushion and a standard issue Amazon desk. The "desk" consisted of a 3 by 6 foot, solid-core wooden door mounted on four 4 by 4 inch legs with a large crack running up at least two of them. At each corner, triangular brackets secured the legs to the door in the direct line of impact with my kneecaps.

To introduce a bit of warmth into this Spartan setup, I installed a small table lamp that cast a pool of yellow light across my desktop. It provided a welcome relief and alternative to the humming fluorescent light overhead. I noticed when people came to visit, they would sit right next to the lamp, like campers huddling close to a campfire on a chilly summer night.

It had been another one of those bone-grinding, brain-growing days when against all odds, our team had brought in its first major fulfillment center deal near Reno, Nevada. Because the whole world was curious about the strategy and odds of success for this scrappy, defiant, and heavily capitalized Internet company, we had to conduct our site acquisition undercover. No real names, addresses, or other personal identifiers were used as we conducted our research, tours, and negotiations.

No one outside the company was allowed to know how Amazon intended to roll out its distribution strategy. The recent addition to Amazon of my first boss there, the chief logistics officer, formerly of Walmart, and his cohort, the chief information officer, also from Walmart, particularly piqued the curiosity of the business world. What those hires signaled to the market was that Amazon had decided to become serious about product distribution. Even inside, the company observed extreme confidentiality.

When asked to find a Reno distribution center, I was informed that only five persons, namely the CEO, chief logistics officer, treasurer, director of operations, and me, were allowed to know about it. No one else in the company, including our chief financial officer, was let in on the secret, which was a bit complicating when I finally had to go ask for money.

Operating under the cover of darkness to secure a 500,000-square-foot distribution center that happened to be immediately available in the then small Reno market added to our already long list of challenges. Industry rumors kept flying around about our whereabouts, which were invariably wrong and distracting. When we finally found a candidate property in the small ranching community of Fernley, Nevada, we could not disclose until the last minute our company identity to the investors who had provisionally committed to purchase the building and rent it back to us. Then we had to hope that the investors and, even more important, their bank would approve the credit of this new and unprofitable company in an unproven industry.

If that was not enough, while we were standing around the building waiting to finalize the deal terms with the investors, we also had to create a physical buffer between the curious plant employees working for the current building tenant and the twenty-four logistics experts the CLO brought in to visit for the day. Without the luxury of time, or a lease for that matter, the experts were there to determine whether the twentieth-century distribution center could be redesigned in six months into a completely new twenty-first-century fulfillment center that could process everything from books to TV sets for individual consumers.

When we finally had the current plant workers segregated from the visitors, the logistics experts tucked into a closed room, and the investors satisfied with the terms of our lease deal, we were ready to fax the nondisclosure agreement to the investors for the "great reveal" of who we actually were. Two minutes before we planned to push the "send" button, all connectivity to the building crashed.

We were in a small Nevada town with few businesses that were not ranch related, so most were unlikely to have fax machines. I stared morosely out of the distribution center window, wondering who might have one. About a half mile away, I spied a Best Western hotel. My bet was that it might have one of those ancient machines that could send one page every eight minutes. I motioned to our broker and we jumped into the car to drive to the hotel. Sure enough, it had a fax machine and a friendly manager who was more than happy to allow us to send a fax at one dollar per page.

Eight pages and eight minutes per page later, to our great surprise and delight we received the blessing for the deal from the investors and their bank. I also discovered while paying for the fax that I had attended junior high school with the hotel manager in the small town of Claremont, California.

Then Came Germany

The acquisition of the Fernley distribution center proved to be a mere introduction to leading in the new world of the twenty-first century. Little did we know at the time that our experience in Fernley would be reinforced in Germany and then become a working template for navigating the unknown.

A few days after our adventure with the hotel fax machine, I was back in my office recovering from the ordeal and basking in the glory of having secured an expandable 323,000-square-foot facility in Fernley, Nevada.

As anyone who has been in business knows, the time interval between the afterglow of celebrating a job well done and "what-have-you-done-for-me-lately?" is about a nanosecond. That night as I sat in my ill-lit office enjoying my glowing nanosecond, the phone rang.

"Julie!" chirped one of my colleagues from Operations calling on behalf of our mutual boss, the CLO. By the abrupt way he uttered my name, I knew this was not a social call. Those were rare enough, but they did occur. No, this was a call to arms for something.

"Julie!" he said again when I failed to answer fast enough. This time he did not wait for a reply. "We need you to go to Germany to find us a 500,000-square-foot distribution center. It has to be tied up by mid-March [1999] and open by August [also 1999]."

"Is that all?"

"That would be all."

The call ended.

By now, I was all too familiar with the tabula rasa nature of requests at Amazon. Business plans were regarded as a bourgeois concept. How can you build a plan with so few tested ingredients? Therefore, most requests came with few to no parameters. Asking where in the whole of Germany the executive team wanted said site was a futile question. Who knew? That was up to me and my team to figure out.

There were also many other things to figure out, as I started ticking off to myself the long list of protests I could already anticipate receiving from other departments:

Finance: How can we possibly achieve market rate rents with such an aggressive timetable?

Human Resources: You have to find a facility near our current operations in Germany so we don't have to move personnel and trigger German law on financial compensation to employees whose place of work moves more than thirty miles away. (Of course, there was nothing even remotely available within 100 miles of the existing German operations.)

Treasury: NO extra travel money for flight reservations made on short notice!

Operations: No way can we put the specs together for that place with all the other things we've got going on!

Legal: How are we going to find reliable German legal counsel on such short notice? You know how much trouble we had in [country name withheld]!

Etc., etc.

That was a mere starter kit of impossibilities with many more to come. I stared into the deep void before me imagining all the roadblocks we would have to surmount and how absolutely stressful that would be. There was so much we did not know. Further, the answers to the foregoing questions would lead to many more questions.

The pursuit of the German distribution center mirrored Fernley, only with even more layers of ambiguity. The facts were different, the themes were the same steady parade of unknowns: new property, new geography, new players, new subsidiary, new team, new culture, new rules (or rather lack thereof), and rampant resistance to most of what we were setting out to do. When answers are not obvious, "No" comes so much more easily than, "I don't know, but let's try it." What I had to do was to not know and still try.

The Epiphany
(or Rather, the Beginning Thereof)

It goes without saying that as I sat in my $129 chair thinking about the towering pile of challenges that night, I felt great anxiety. With Fernley fresh in mind, I knew that every step of the way would be uncharted and crazy. I like to push the edges and convert impossibilities into possibilities, but even I have my limits. Then, I noticed something else.

No matter how anxious I felt about tying up a large German distribution center in less than two months, there was no part of me that did not believe we could pull it off. I didn't know how. I only knew we would.

Then I sensed an equally strong feeling. Despite all my anxiety, I was okay with the scariness of it all. Part of me was actually excited by the prospect of going after this assignment with all its unknowns.

What that meant for leadership came to me later when I thought back to that night. For now, I had to go to work, leading the acquisition of a German distribution center at warp speed. That meant solving how to move from a new A to a new Z.

The First Step into the Unknown: Finding Our Way through the Fog

Our first dive into the unknown on this initiative turned out to be finding the Amazon office in Germany.

As if following my imagined internal script of impossibilities, Treasury opposed approving extra dollars for air travel on short notice. After making a personal visit to Treasury, we procured two seats for our industrial real estate broker and me to fly to Munich, Germany. The broker had been one of the bright lights in the tunnel of resistance during our Nevada distribution center acquisition, because of her willingness to work with few known quantities.

Our mission was to travel to Regensburg, Germany, home of Amazon.de, the recently acquired Amazon German online bookstore, Telebuch.de. There we planned to meet with its general manager and cofounder, a freshly minted multimillionaire (courtesy of the acquisition of his company by Amazon.com) to discuss how to move his operation far from its current office and warehouse to some place on the other side of Germany with a 500,000-square-foot distribution center. I did not know this person, or he me, and neither of us was looking forward to our first encounter.

After twenty-four hours of budget travel that took us late at night through an empty, foodless, Chicago O'Hare International Airport, we arrived the next morning in Munich. The car rental agency provided us with a small, black, two-slice toaster they claimed was a Mercedes and a map showing us how to drive from the airport to the immediately adjacent autoroute. We were too tired and disoriented to ask for more.

Before we hit the autoroute, I shook off my mental haze long enough to call the Amazon.de office for navigational assistance. The staff member who answered rattled off in a strong German accent a set of directions from Munich to Amazon.de in Regensburg. Unfortunately, about three-quarters of the way through his explanation I quit listening. I would like to say that my jet lag had taken over. In truth, I was tired, hungry, and annoyed that we had spent an extra fifteen minutes in the rental car garage at the broker's insistence to report a ding in the toaster's right rear fender (and perhaps to empty the crumb tray?).

I relayed to our broker as she returned from the rental car desk that I had directions to Regensburg.

"So, where do we go when we get into Regensburg?"

"I stopped listening at that point."

"You 'stopped listening'?"

"I got bored." I confess to less-than-exemplary behavior at times, and this was one of those times. Understandably our broker was not pleased, but off we went to the autoroute.

We got as far as the Regensburg city limits. As we crossed the border, a thick fog symbolically descended, obscuring all but the largest traffic signs. By now I realized that without knowing German, matching street signs to verbal instructions was hopeless. We needed a personal escort. But how could we tell anyone where to find us when we did not know where we were?

I started thinking about which global franchises would have the best site acquisition people. Those would be the ones who knew where to locate a store close to the autoroute that all the citizens of Regensburg could easily find (and patronize). The answer: McDonald's. Sure enough, as if the heavens heard my plea, a McDonald's restaurant miraculously appeared to the left of us, across the highway. We banked onto the exit ramp and landed at McDonald's, frazzled but thrilled.

Having visited Europe many times before, I expected, entering one of America's favorite formula restaurants, that its German version would contain tables of Europeans sitting in groups of twos and threes, working slowly through their lunches while carrying on long, meaningful conversations.

Instead, we stepped out of the gray fog into the Star Wars Mos Eisley Cantina. Before us lay a dingy, chopped-up room with a broad assortment of oddly shaped clientele. Some stood and others sat at tables angled in random directions. They talked loudly, greasy food oscillating in their mouths. A few did not eat but merely watched in silence while their children tore up the room. Everyone spoke English with thick American accents. In the United States, this would have felt normal. In Germany . . . well, it did little to lift our disorientation. We learned later an American Army base was nearby.

Hungry as we were, we decided to pass on lunch. I retreated to the edge of the room to call the Amazon.de office to ask if anyone there knew the place and could he or she provide us with a pilot car? Sure enough, the McDonald's site acquisition people had done their homework. Without hesitation, our German colleague responded, "Of course," and ten minutes later our local representative materialized.

I would like to say that from there on, it was smooth sailing. Nothing could have been further from the truth. Overcoming our brief navigation odyssey was a nothing. The real tests lay ahead.

The Second Step into the Unknown: Finding Our Way into the Hearts and Minds of Amazon.de

The first real test involved winning the hearts and minds of a team I had never met to support a new base of operations, leadership, and operational systems. No one could predict how that was to go. Amazon.com might have shipped to more than 160 countries, but understanding the work cultures of geographies outside the United States was something else. So far, one could best describe the relationships with our overseas colleagues as "tenuous."

The former Telebuch.de workers liked their independence and, similar to any subsidiary, new or old, were not predisposed to taking direction from outsiders, including their new parent company. As the Seattle-based director of global real estate, I could easily be swept into their outsider category. Yet without the real estate we were there to procure (and finance), they had no place from which to ship books to meet their rapidly expanding customer base.

I do not sleep well on airplanes and by the time we arrived at the Amazon.de offices, I had been awake for most of the preceding thirty hours. Once we escaped McDonald's and arrived at the Amazon.de offices, a young German worker showed us into a large, dark brown room. At the far end of it stood the tall, impeccably dressed Amazon.de country manager. He nodded stiffly and welcomed us in precise, chilly English.

Even in my travel-induced stupor, I knew this was not the moment to assert corporate headquarters authority. I glanced briefly around the room. It bore all the usual trappings of a startup—random pieces of used furniture, nothing on the walls, and a large table filling out the center of the room where all business took place. Outside the office was a large drafty space with a handful of desks and a few workers moving quietly among them to enter the warehouse adjacent to it.

Nothing I saw suggested that anyone from Amazon headquarters in Seattle had ever been there. Had they been there, I would have seen a fleet of door desks covered in monitors with Amazonians leaned over them furiously typing. The hallways would have been festooned with monster-sized pieces of computer paper, covered with code. Instead, all I saw were blank, beige walls as I walked through the space.

In fact, headquarters people had spent a lot of time at the site, and I heard things had not gone well. After its acquisition of Telebuch.de, Amazon.com had to rebuild the systems of its new subsidiary to handle exponential expansion beyond the borders of Germany. As anyone who has been through a corporate acquisition knows, integration is stressful at the best of times. The major overhaul of what the German company employees had worked hard to create had been painful, particularly for its founders.

It would have been easy to take the German general manager's cool behavior personally. After all, he was glaring directly at me. I resisted the twinge of feeling devalued. After all, how could this possibly be personal? We had communicated only briefly by email. More likely, I thought, he viewed me as another corporate shill coming to tell him what to do.

That was a guess. I really had no idea what he thought. I did know that somehow we had to establish some trust quickly if we were going to find in the next twenty-four hours a large, yet undiscovered, piece of real estate essential to his business. I also disliked the prospect of being thwarted by a bad attitude for which I was not responsible. That last feeling, I kept to myself, although it informed my next move. I decided I had better find out what I did not know, which was a lot.

The Broader Landscape of Unknowns in 1999: The Map with No Fixed Points . . . Anywhere

Our department vision at Amazon was to develop and manage a right-sized, timed, and located global real estate portfolio that would carry out the company business strategy. Fernley was the first major foray toward this goal. Germany would be the second. Success was important to house the steady increase in headcount and functions resulting from explosive company growth. We also needed it to build political capital to realize our vision. Focusing on that helped me to sort out my priorities and come up with a strategy for establishing trust with the Germany country manager.

There were also many other issues we had to address to win in Germany. As was common among their counterparts at other companies, Amazon senior executives regarded real estate as a necessary evil, because unless a company ties up a large amount of capital to buy it (an unpopular strategy), it costs significant money to occupy and does not generate any. Winning the buy-in on the many multimillion-dollar decisions required for a large global portfolio of "necessary evil" meant a large quantity of political work to convince the approver du jour (which changed constantly based on no discernible principle) that there was a good reason to lease sizable pieces of real estate.

I was used to advocacy after working many years as a finance lawyer and real estate developer. Arguing for things came naturally. However, that willingness to advocate presupposed I had the usual business planning tools to make a case for large real estate lease commitments. Corporate real estate acquisition customarily starts with an assessment of business requirements. Early Amazon had no appetite for conventional planning. We had no operating history to inform our decisions, no official business plans or forecasts to allow us to plan our real estate systematically or even strategies to create them. Our CEO, Jeff Bezos, a man with a deep intellectual curiosity and inclination toward libertarian values, thrived on the new and the inventive. That was our only template.

I was good with that. I like to invent. That did not make it easy. It kept me on the edge most of the time, because we had to keep creating both simple and complicated things to solve problems that were not relevant in other companies (yet) or had been done many times before. The German distribution center initiative occurred early in our history at Amazon. At that time, we did not even have an official company capital budget. My department discovered that small fact in late 1998 when we were about to spend twenty million dollars to convert an Art Deco veterans' hospital on a hilltop south of downtown Seattle into a 184,000-square-foot corporate head-quarters building.

One of the benefits of working for a libertarian, or at least our libertarian, was that if you made bold, smart moves, there were few barriers to action. That had its pluses and minuses. In the case of our need for capital, it was a definite plus. We simply went ahead and developed the first company capital budget, expense report, and, after the German distribution center acquisition, integrated strategic planning group that the department leaders from the rest of the company quickly joined.

With few procedures in place, or at best, constantly changing ones, a vital tool I had at my disposal in Germany was a high pain threshold. It allowed me to face multiple personal agendas and walls of resistance at all levels as I worked to uncover what we needed to know to succeed in our mission.

I thought our first challenge would be to build an ad hoc business case. It turns out that was the least of my worries. While we still had to piece together a strategy to determine the size, phasing, and location of a facility, in this hunt we had the distinct benefit of a CEO who had ordered his direct reports in general and my manager, the chief logistics officer, in particular to deliver a major distribution center expansion for 1999. Therefore, no official company business case for the facility would be required, at least this time around.

That helped with plane ticket approvals. However, that did not make it so with all the human factors lying on the ground where the actual implementation of the CEO's imperative had to take place. Therein rose the many rivers to cross.

Among other things, in the pursuit of its new distribution center we were asking the German staff, with whom we had no track record, to move across the country. Consultants were requested to compress their customary long processes but maintain their level of quality, and finance people had to fund a large real estate acquisition when most of them had never met real estate except to record rental payments into the general ledger.

Outside the company, we had to convince an unfamiliar German property owner to lease to us a large distribution center, with us paying rent from a relatively new income stream. When acquiring property in the United States, we were helped by the excitement and curiosity that Amazon evoked. By this time, we were the darlings of the American press. No day went by without considerable coverage.

Buying things on the Internet was in its infancy, yet it was an infant that mesmerized Wall Street and touched enough people in the country to give us some benefit of the doubt. In Europe, ecommerce was brand new. Few outside the financial sector had heard of us, much less cared. That meant we stood to receive little to no benefit of the doubt in Europe, and there was a serious doubt as to whether we could perform.

Nevertheless, the charge from our American parent company was exactly that, "perform." Operations wanted its distribution center open by August 1999. Finance wanted us not to spend much money because Wall Street was asking for more fiscal restraint. The rest of the Amazon employees yearned for a modicum of sanity to build a 500,000-square-foot warehouse in four months, install a twenty-first-century fulfillment system, and fill the building with products to ship for Christmas 1999.

This was my backdrop, and it was a daunting one. Nevertheless, there was no choice but to focus on the moment and move forward, one step at a time.

Returning to the Second Step into the Unknown: Breaking through to Amazon.de

Back in the Amazon.de office, I had settled into our situation. I needed first to know who this person was and what he wanted. I looked directly at the country manager. Addressing him by name, I said, "I am here to learn. I don't know anything about your business or its operations. What I need is for you to educate me, so I can help you get what you need."

What I believe made a difference was that I meant what I said. There was no way I could solve his problems without knowing what they were. I also found compassion for him. Even with a large check from Amazon to purchase his company, giving up his autonomy and authority over the enterprise he had built could not have been entirely easy.

He said nothing for a minute. Then his demeanor shifted. He looked both surprised and relieved. His shoulders relaxed, he smiled, and then started to talk.

For the next two hours, he told us about how he built his online bookselling company, what happened when Amazon.com came calling, and what he needed now. At the end of that conversation, I had learned what I needed about the business needs of Amazon.de. Even more important, I learned what mattered to him. It made a difference to both of us.

The details of that conversation have faded over time. They included many dates and data points on how the business began, its past rate of growth, and opinions on how much of the German book market could be captured by online sales during the next five to ten years. What remains of the conversation most is the strong impression of hearing someone who was proud of what he built and wanted recognition for creating something that a company like Amazon wanted to buy.

Too often, once a company is acquired, what it took to make it saleable is forgotten as people shift their attention to the new organization. The need of the country manager to talk and me to listen put in place an important first building block for our hyper-paced pursuit of a large distribution center.

Back into the Fog: The Pursuit of Property

The next day at the crack of dawn, we assembled in our hotel parking lot with the country manager and our German brokers. Our objective was to drive across the country to tour the handful of distribution centers that were both large and immediately available. Returning to the metaphor of the day before, a thick curtain of fog dropped around us as we exited the parking lot, leaving about 100 feet of visibility.

Further testing my fortitude, the country manager led the way in his Porsche, driving at a speed well north of 100 mph. I thought this was rather plucky since I had heard he had only recently regained his driver's license after a two-month suspension for driving 140 mph late one autumn night. I sank my fingers deep into the fancy leather upholstery of the broker's car in which I sat and off we flew to catch up with the Porsche.

Our tour took us to the environs of Frankfurt through four different sites of various designs and dimensions. Each of them was too big, too strangely configured, or too isolated. Then we came to the last stop on our tour, Bad Hersfeld, a beautiful, small town ninety miles north of Frankfurt. Right inside the city limits lay a large, green field waiting for someone to build a distribution center on it. The small municipality of about 30,000 people hoped that "someone" would be Amazon.com.

We had at most two months to close a complicated deal and four more months to build out a fully functioning twenty-first-century distribution center. The permits alone could consume at least half that total time frame. At the invitation of the Bad Hersfeld mayor, we drove to the town hall to meet with him and his staff to learn how they proposed to help us with our time crunch. The room at the town hall was filled to capacity with about twenty-five people, including the mayor, his staff, the green field property owners, and us. No one spoke English other than our tour group.

I sat at the edge of the room, with our German broker whispering a rough English translation into my ear, giving me the gist of the mayor's remarks. In essence, the town committed to expedite all permits to deliver the building on time. There still was much to overcome, given our schedule, but it was a good start, if they could really do it.

Without any other properties showing promise, the Bad Hersfeld site, with its near impossible schedule, was our only choice. Toward that end, we immediately released an army of project managers, architects, engineers, contractors, and logistics experts to undertake the due diligence and prepare for a construction miracle.

Building a (Large) Fulfillment Center before Christmas, and a Team to Get There

Intense activity ensued. Real Estate, Engineering, and Operations people threw themselves onto airplanes to evaluate the property, architects dived into CAD programs, industrial engineers generated countless fulfillment center designs, and construction people gnashed their way through German building codes. Legal found the outside counsel it needed and speedily drafted us a letter of intent to catalyze the next set of the steps. Human Resources dug into researching how to move and augment a workforce 220 miles from Regensburg. IT hunkered down to work out how to create a major fiber connection to that small German town. The Bad Hersfeld town staff, true to the mayor's word, proved to be highly accommodating.

Aside from negotiating the real estate deal with the owner, my biggest job was to manage the constant stress felt by everyone on the team, whose membership changed daily. Exciting as a project of this magnitude and schedule was, there remained the reality that it had many things that had not been done before, at our company or elsewhere.

We were making decisions with best guesses to questions like these:

- How do you size a distribution floor and power panel when you really have no idea how many books people will be willing to buy online and no history as a guide?
- How do you phase construction of a large building when you have no idea of the same details?
- How do you hire many people to come work at a brand new company in a brand new industry?
- How do you figure out the economics of a real estate transaction where no other comparable transactions are available in the area?

Where there is high speed, high stakes, and high ambiguity, anxiety rules the day. We lived on a constant learning curve. Not only were we learning how to conduct business overseas with all the "new" things we faced, we had the almost daily addition of new people showing up whose personal agendas had to be uncovered and managed. When a company has few processes, personalities prevail. Knowing personal agendas is always relevant, even more so when everything is new. Some agendas are easily decoded. Others are not. When there are no institutional or personal histories on which to rely, everything resides in the unknown.

I spent most of my time finding out how little people knew about Amazon, explaining to them who we were, mediating disputes (rational and otherwise), and assuaging the fears of our team members, both employees and consultants. To do that I had to encourage each person, one at a time, to identify the source of his or her fears, however deeply they went, and to find a personal motivator to move through all the scariness of constant change.

With so much at stake, there was enormous pressure for everyone to bring their "A" game. We were there to achieve miracles in the brave new world of building bricks and mortar on bits-and-bytes time. It was impossible for it not to cause fear and anger, even with the thrill of the new.

One phone call in particular captured the emotional reactivity of that era. It came from a senior engineering consultant whose name I knew, but whom I had not met until he called me out of the blue.

"Julie!" came a voice in a refined, upper-crust, English accent. He gave his name and the name of his company. "Wait a minute. I need to sit down." He grunted as he found someplace to sit. "Okay. I am now teetering on the edge of a curb cut near this (here, he threw out the first in a series of F bombs) site."

What followed was a string of more variations of the F word than I knew existed, even with the benefit of having attended an esteemed women's college. The actual complaints mattered little, to him or to me. They ranged from annoyance with unavailability of supplies to [expletive deleted] subcontractors who could not read [another expletive deleted] blueprints. I gathered he just needed to vent. At the end of his stream of invective, we simultaneously burst into laughter, wished each other good luck, and went back to our respective days.

Chaos continued to abound, but we muscled our way through it, unraveling issues one by one, fighting each battle as it came, or if we were prescient, before it arrived. Stressful as it was, things looked promising.

The Defining Leadership Moment: Part 1—The Stranger on the Phone

I did not expect the defining leadership moment for the German initiative would come when we needed Finance to approve our final letter of intent.

As is the custom of startup companies, things happen in scrums. When there is a pending decision, everyone piles on, whether or not they belong in the fray. When it came time to ask Finance for its approval, someone from that department summoned us to attend a conference call. The list of attendees included about ten people located in several different Amazon offices around downtown Seattle and twenty Amazon employees and consultants in a conference room in Germany. No one knew who was leading the call—only that the Finance Department had scheduled it.

I cannot remember who opened the meeting, probably because it quickly became irrelevant. Two sentences into the call, we heard an unidentified male voice. He offered no name or anything else by way of introduction, and the Meeting Maker scheduling tool provided no clues. With an oily, sarcastic voice, he launched into giving us the third degree.

"Well, how do you know these rental rates are market rates?" We explained how the brokers had collected information from recent transactions that corresponded as closely as possible to our proposed transaction. With no comparable transactions in the area, we had to extrapolate from neighboring geographies. This was not an unusual approach when entering new geographies.

"So, what makes you think what they gave you is reliable?" The volume of his voice ticked up a notch. We described how real estate brokers made it their business to collect information from the front line of the market on an ongoing basis, without which they could not close deals. We went on to tell him more on how they sourced that data.

And on it went. I resisted reciprocating his sarcasm, sorely tempting as that was with someone more interested in taking shots than listening. I decided to spend my energy figuring out what strategy to use on this call. That was tough, because I still had no idea who he was, and I thought I knew the Finance Department well.

While half listening to this stranger's next verbal assault, I emailed one of my Finance cohorts who I knew was on the call, asking, "Who the hell is this guy?" What came back was, "Our newest finance exec." Wonderful.

Mr. Newest Finance Exec, his voice growing even louder, was now asking why we had not conducted a full-scale rental market study.

We responded that our schedule and the practicalities of the German real estate industry did not allow for it. There were more than sixty regional markets in Germany and no integrated report existed that included all of them. In addition, in 1999, the former West Germany was still struggling with how to work with the former East Germany. Many West Germans felt aggrieved that they had to subsidize their reunified neighbor. Information flow was not a priority. Instead, we had to rely on German real estate professionals from the central German region to give us the best market information available. They had their own reputation to protect. It did not behoove them to make things up, since eventually the truth would be known.

We then talked about our primary focus on what was knowable: making sure the property owner would not make more than a commercially reasonable economic return. Reasonable economic returns were well understood and verifiable by both the real estate industry and Amazon.

At this juncture, this stranger to us and, obviously, real estate, thundered over the phone, "Well, that is NOT going to work. We have to have better information. Shame on you, Facilities, SHAME on you for not doing your homework!!"

Everyone on the call sat in stunned silence. That included me. Had he really said that? I have certainly had angry moments in my professional life, but usually can move quickly beyond their sting to action. Twice, however (once with a used car dealer and now with this new finance executive), I became so enraged that the room became vault-like still and flashed into two dimensions. Everything around me looked flat. My senior manager of Project Management, who was the only other person in the room with me, watched my expression as I sorted through my thoughts.

The Defining Leadership Moment:
Part 2—Accessing My Core

I did not know this new finance executive, his work history, personal style, motivators . . . I did not even know his name, since still none had been offered. In that ugly moment on the conference call with an audience of more than thirty people, there was no time to find out. What I did know was that his last comment crossed the line. He had violated my value system.

As a leader, you have to know who you are and for what you stand. You have to know your values, personal history, and dreams for the future. When living in the world of unknowns, knowing yourself gives you guiding lights, your core drivers to move you through the scariness of all the ambiguity that is your daily fare as a leader.

One of the things I knew on that conference call was that I hold a deep personal value that it is totally unacceptable to insult people who are working hard for you and doing their best to deliver. I also do not tolerate that behavior in others, especially with a blaze of uninformed accusations, such as the ones coming from the stranger on the phone.

I took a page from my mother's book. She could stand down anyone with her firm resolve fueled by values that had allowed her to hold her ground during an era when those in her socio-economic circle assumed she had none on which to stand. I became steely calm, leaned into the speakerphone, and said in a level voice,

"I am disconcerted with the tenor of this call. We are here to work together to make this deal happen. We have been asked to deliver a large facility on an unprecedented schedule. To accomplish that we have to do our homework, and doing it we are. That does not mean we can do everything we would like to do. However, we are not going to cut any corners that should not be cut. Jeff Bezos' mandate for this deal is for delivery in March. If you don't like the schedule, you can go talk to him."

After I finished, my senior manager for Project Management jumped in to remind this stranger of a fundamental principle of project management. "In a project, you have three things—scope, time, and cost. You can give on one or two, but you can never give on all three!"

Later, I was told that at this juncture, the German conference room exploded with twenty pairs of arms flying into the air and everyone mouthing the word, "Score!"

I don't know what the new finance executive thought, except that he suddenly became ultra-polite. A few days after the call, the deal got approved with little more asked from us.

I felt proud of having been not only true to myself but also for letting others know my values as a leader and how I expected people to behave. Even more, I was immensely proud of the team for all their hard work and willingness to maintain focus on the bigger goal of delivering, despite all the changing conditions, a large distribution center for Christmas.

The Aftermath

Right after the Finance conference call, I received phone calls from two different executives in that department who had been listening in. They both told me how awful they thought their new colleague had acted, obviously wanting to distance themselves as fast as possible from his obnoxious, politically questionable behavior. To be fair, after his unfortunate debut, once the new finance executive settled into his new role, he turned out to be a reasonable person.

As in all things, crisis leads to opportunity. What we learned from this event was we needed a vehicle to approve deals by applying a little more orthodoxy to the process, even in an ever-changing, libertarian-run company. With the help of a timely suggestion from our director of Tax, the Real Estate SWAT was born. Real Estate SWAT provided a cross-functional, executive-level, strategic-planning engine that would meet on a weekly basis for one hour to review and approve all real estate deals. It allowed all of us to combine what we knew with what we needed to learn to make reasonably informed decisions in our fast-moving environment.

We closed more than twenty-six deals during my first year at Amazon, and in two years spent more than $320 million on seven million square feet of real estate worldwide. We had plenty to do. Real Estate SWAT lasted almost two years, at which time planning as an official process appeared in the company.

We also delivered a fully operational German distribution center to ship products in time for Christmas 1999.

What I Learned about Leadership and the Unknown One Night in January 1999

Before Amazon

Before Amazon, I equated leadership with strategy. From my own experience as a leader, I had long embraced the idea that leadership requires a strategic mindset, one that perpetually seeks the larger opportunity that arises from every operational moment.

In the foreground of organizational life travels a constant flow of operational challenges that need attention. In the background is a larger system that requires even more attention. The leadership mindset means focusing on the background implications of what is happening in the foreground.

I trademarked the term Dual Screen Management® to encapsulate the idea that every operational issue has a strategic opportunity. The "dual screen" refers to a metaphorical image of two different windows open on a computer. On the first is the information about an operational problem that needs to be solved. On the second is an empty screen that can be filled by an executive simultaneously with a larger, more strategic solution for the operational issue to prevent its recurrence.

For example, a finance director who is routinely late in delivering quarterly reports to senior management might lack good workload management skills. He also might be late because of a wider, more strategic issue.

Smart leaders use the stress caused by operational issues as an opportunity to explore broader solutions. Closer scrutiny might reveal more systemic issues that can be addressed at a strategic level. In the case of the finance director, the resistance to releasing reports might come from his knowledge that the information included in the report from other departments is flawed. That could point to an issue of company standards regarding its information integrity. He might also know that the company has a tendency to shoot the messenger, which suggests a problem with the company's culture of accountability.

Another possibility could be, as I discovered during a consulting project, that the finance director's skillset could not meet the needs of a new organizational strategy. His inability to deliver reports on time was caused by his lack of training for the financial issues now faced under the new strategic plan.

When they examined the larger picture, the company leaders with whom I consulted solved the strategic issue, aligning their financial leadership with their strategic direction. They restructured the finance function, adding a CFO position at the top and finding another more appropriate role for the current senior finance person. Then they hired someone qualified for the new CFO role.

After Amazon

After my experience at Amazon, I realized defining leadership as a mindset that embraced Dual Screen Management was not enough. It was missing an essential ingredient.

In trying to capture the je ne sais quoi of leadership, I thought back to that night at Amazon in January 1999 when I received the call to go to Germany.

With the benefit of what went on at Amazon, before and many times after that night, I grasped what the missing key ingredient was. It is the deeply visceral aspect of being a leader. In plunging into the unknown world of new ideas and relationships to build something better, a leader must confront and accept the fundamental scariness of it.

In other words, to be a leader means having a frame of mind that is propelled to build something better *AND is comfortable with the discomfort of not knowing.* That is the leadership mindset.

Accepting the discomfort of not knowing all the answers distinguishes leadership from all other governing roles in an organization. To reach those untried strategic ideas that improve the future of people, organizations, and things, a leader must be okay with the scariness that new frontiers can bring.

What I subliminally realized while sitting in my Amazon office one night in January 1999 was for all the answers I had to find, I knew a great deal about who I was and ultimately what I wanted to achieve. That gave me the ballast to be comfortable with the constant discomfort I felt anticipating all the situational and interpersonal unknowns that lay ahead in Germany and the many initiatives that followed.

Learning to master navigation of the unknown and to accept its scariness as inspiration rather than deterrent taught me about the essential link between leadership and the unknown, especially in the twenty-first century.

Part 2

LEADERSHIP AND THE UNKNOWN

LEADERSHIP IS NOT like any other job. In fact, you might not even call it a job. It has general requirements—create a vision, serve your stakeholders, and build an organization to deliver those things. However, rather than being a position with a long list of functional responsibilities, leadership more accurately can be described as a mindset. It is a way of being that reflects how you view the world, who you are, and what you want to do in and for it.

What Leadership (Really) Is

Evening in an office ushers in an odd tranquility. With the departure of the workforce, the daily hubbub of conversation, machine noise, and human movement ceases. The scene changes to a few remaining workers who hunch over their desks absorbed in projects or quiet conversations with one another. The atmosphere is one of enveloping calm and deep concentration.

For an executive, evening has a different breed of quiet. Without employees, vendors, or investors filling the doorframe, it can present a moment of disconcerting emptiness. The usual distractions of the business day that so automatically structure the time disappear. No one is around to ask for input, bring up a new problem, or harp on an organizational complaint.

At this moment arrives a critical choice. Always in plain view loom unsorted emails, reports, and requests beckoning executive attention. Indeed, such items require attention, and doing things that need doing does move things forward. The feeling of satisfaction that comes with checking things off a list is hard to resist.

It is just that spending valuable time on them does not take the organization to a new and better place, a place yet to be discovered.

Leadership, put simply, is about discovering strategic ideas that lift an organization to a better place and bringing others along to make them happen. It takes you away from the well-worn, prescribed routines of business life into corridors not seen before, unknown places that hold endless promise, ambiguity, and trepidation.

Winning means generating ideas that move the business into the future to improve the lives of customers, employees, shareholders, and communities. Between producing ideas and delivering them lies the reality of daily business life, an obstacle course of personal and organizational hurdles that can make it tough to achieve results. By their nature, new ideas are hard to make real. That is what makes them so compelling. Furthermore, as the ideas evolve, leaders also evolve to want more and better for their organizations.

Leaders succeed by stepping into new places without the benefit of a clear roadmap, and convincing others to join as they create a route. The courage to do that has to come from them. It is not for everyone, yet to understand its properties can open the door to deep professional and personal rewards.

Leadership offers those who choose it an opportunity to have an impact on people's lives. Driving the urge to lead is a hunger rising out of life history, dreams, and personal values to find untried ideas that will make a positive difference.

To satisfy that hunger, a leader enters a large labyrinth of unfamiliar, dimly lit corridors of endless questions and choices. The corridors twist, turn, and exit at some yet-to-be-known place. It can feel inefficient, unfamiliar, and anxiety provoking. Yet in those twists and turns lies a journey toward the possibilities of something different, bigger, better.

The journey through those corridors is intense; a leader ultimately takes the journey alone. When you are a leader, you lead the expedition that others might or might not want to join. Generating visions for better futures can feel exhilarating. At the same time, what is hard to fathom is that while you are exploring the scary place of new ideas, not everyone will want to spend time there with you. That is because when you embark on the leader's journey—leaning forward, tilting at windmills—it is anything but comfortable. It comes with no promise of success, or even failure.

In short, the future of new ideas is unknown, and that makes all the difference.

What Leadership Is Not

Leadership is not management, although it shares with management a strong interest in effective execution and the generation of profit. Management follows a different trajectory from leadership. Management is the fine art and science of making sure the daily things are done. It is critical to the ongoing operation of a business, the generation of revenue, and the delivery of company strategy. Its responsibilities, while vast, are nevertheless finite. There is a list of things to accomplish and agreed deliverables. Success is understood. The budget is completed and implemented. A report is distributed to stakeholders. Staffing plans go out to the relevant managers for review and application.

The job of the manager is to organize and implement. It has an elemental tidiness to it. As seasoned managers will tell you, their main job is "to make order out of chaos." This job description does not mean managing is not stressful. Juggling the competing demands of budget, headcount, diverse department plans, and financial stakeholders can be difficult. However, the methods of balancing a budget and delivering on its line items are ultimately understood. The challenge rests in how to apply rather than create them.

In short, for management the pathway to success is known.

Leadership is also not the delivery of deals or the management of projects. Many executives see their leadership roles as being lead-deal jockeys or project junkies. There is no doubt that deals and project execution require a high level of expertise. They also have many scary moments. Ultimately, however, those pathways are also known.

In a deal, there are only so many ways to arrive at a price or interpret an indemnification clause. Intellectual and emotional land mines riddle the road to agreement, but there is a known repertoire of solutions. The source of stress in a deal comes more from its choreography. How fast or slow will the other party reveal its needs? What will be the pitch of his or her voice? Who else has to be brought into the room?

In projects, creating a budget with less than robust cash flow and many expense lines is definitely stressful. Finding the right combination of expense allocations and reasonable assumptions about future revenue requires both skill and courage. Ultimately, however, the person creating the budget knows how to apply the relevant tools to establish salary levels, market rental rates, and the range of foreseeable sales based on past results and industry performance. Driving a schedule to hit critical milestones can be nerve-wracking, but deciding on whom to involve is a familiar course. Again, the road to delivering budgets and schedules is known.

There is no doubt that deals and projects hold critical importance to an organization. After all, they generate the revenue that makes things go. To grow, however, a company must project into the future what its customers, employees, and funders will need and want. As those needs and wants change, so too must the company business growth strategy. That requires trying new things to match the evolving needs of its stakeholders. Those new things reside in the world of the unknown, the world where leaders must live.

The Labyrinth of Leadership

Leadership follows a different and more circuitous route from managing and deal making.

Imagine yourself standing at the opening of a tall, large labyrinth with multiple corridors, limited lighting, and no signage. When you peer into the first corridor, all you see is darkness, or, at best, a tiny bit of light. Your mission is to enter the labyrinth and move along its first corridor. You do not know what is at the end. What you do know is that when you reach it, you will have to make a decision. Do you turn left or right, or do you simply back out of the corridor and move away from the labyrinth completely?

As the leader, your job is to enter that labyrinth with all its unknown hallways. Once you cross its threshold, you will not know the precise roadmap to the exit, and the possible routes seem infinite. What you do know is that an exit exists somewhere. That exit leads to new possibilities, big and small. These possibilities are your "bigger bets," those strategic ideas that lead to a stronger, more successful organization. Achieving them is not easy. The bigger the bet, the larger the labyrinth, and the greater the navigational challenge. Many unknowns line those corridors.

Bigger Bets

The primary function of a leader is to pursue new strategic ideas or "bigger bets." Bigger bets might or might not change the course of life, but their goals are to make things for their stakeholders better—better than what they were. Whether it is a product that is more intuitive and simpler to use for the technologically challenged consumer, a substance that provides a good nutritional alternative to people who are allergic to a common ingredient, or a process that helps people move more purposefully through an organization, the role of a leader is to make things better, not best, but better. *Best* suggests an endpoint, and there is always room for evolution as needs change.

Better means that something different might result. What actually results is unknown until you try it. A bigger bet is not what is right in front of you or business as usual. Rather, it is about what business could be, whether you are talking about strategic positioning, market penetration, flawless execution, or a strong culture that supports the mission.

Bigger bets by their nature are untried and therefore come with risks. They force people to move into an area that is new. Parts of what they experience might be familiar, but for a bigger bet to be, well, bigger, there has to be something about it that is new and unproven.

Finding the answers to these questions is not easy. Successful leaders spend all their time relentlessly scouring unknown corridors in search of patterns and connecting dots that will move the organization beyond the status quo. What product and services should they invent and sell? What work culture will enable excellence and attract top talent? What reputation must they build in the market? How do they keep ahead of customer demand?

Once a critical need is identified, the leaders work through those corridors to find an exit to a better place. It is by no means assured that a better place will appear. Along the way, new facts and forces will challenge the bigger bet and mold the eventual result. It could lead to abandonment of the idea. It also could lead to success, if the leader continues on the journey, repositioning when needed at each new twist and turn.

The Dead-End Corridors: The Gift of Failure

The risk of an unsuccessful outcome might tempt a leader to back out of the labyrinth altogether to the safer territory of known results. Strong as that temptation might be, successful leaders push forward. They are driven by a need to have an impact, even when faced with the possibility of failure.

The road to success is paved with failures. Henry Ford, known for his innovative assembly line and American-made cars, experienced several business failures that left him broke five times before establishing the Ford Motor Company. R. H. Macy had seven failed stores before opening his icon department store in New York City. Akio Morita started Sony Corporation with a rice cooker as its first product. Rather than cook rice, it actually burned it. The company sold fewer than 100 units.

More recent history provides many examples of leaders seeing something others could not, which ultimately led to highly successful results.

- Bill Gates and Paul Allen saw the power of having a "PC on every desk" and how developing software for that personal computer (PC) could create a global business at a time when few people had even heard the word "computer."
- Steve Jobs came up with the iPod during the 2001 recession, saying that he wanted to create products that fulfilled a desire that consumers did not even know they had . . . yet.
- Brian Chesky, Nathan Blecharczyk, and Joe Gebbia, founders of Airbnb, thought there might be a market of global travelers who would prefer the adventure of staying in the private homes of total strangers rather than in commercial hotels.
- Nelson Mandela saw a possibility to unite all South Africans, regardless of color, by competing as "one South Africa" for the Rugby World Cup, at a time when black South Africans hated the sport because of its identification with white South Africans.

What the stories about such bold initiatives fail to mention is that the individuals who came up with these bigger bets, while smart and sure of many things, *had no idea whether or how their ideas would work.* The public has a nasty habit of not sharing its opinions until the people see the goods, and many "goods" have been rejected. Others took off beyond anyone's wildest imagination.

- Initial reviewers saw the iPad as an odd device that did not fit into any particular category of consumer demand, and they assumed it would not find any. Instead, the product created its own category, once consumers got ahold of it and found many reasons for owning one, particularly as the apps marketed exploded in response to the device.

- WD-40 spray was so named because it took forty attempts to make it into a successful degreaser and rust-protection product. Originally used in the aerospace industry, it became so popular with employees that the company finally packaged it in an aerosol can and introduced it to the retail industry.

- Two inventors created bubble wrap in the late 1950s as a trendy modern wallpaper. The public rejected it. It then was offered as housing insulation. That too failed. It was not until IBM began shipping its computer equipment with bubble wrap around it for protection that the product found its niche and took off.

In each case, the rest is history, the end result being quite different from what was originally predicted.

What distinguishes these leaders and the many other pioneers like them was their willingness to navigate through those corridors, no matter how scary. What they had was the drive and emotional fortitude to move through those hallways, lighting them a section at a time while they tried out their ideas.

In other words, they could deal with not knowing.

Working through the labyrinth with all its hallways in pursuit of a bigger bet can feel like a forever proposition. Yet people who want to lead cannot help themselves. Whatever the idea, the need for it creates a strong sensation they cannot ignore. It is an itch that has to be scratched, a wound that must be healed, something that needs to become true. It also takes courage.

They might or might not have been born with a need to lead. People can come into leadership by either deliberate or accidental pathways. They might arrive in the role as part of a methodical succession plan that places them in the leadership role at a designated time. They also might find themselves unexpectedly in a leadership position as the result of a failed succession plan, the sudden departure of an executive due to a medical emergency, or through the act of an acquiring company that elevates the position of a company manager to the executive suite.

Regardless of how they enter leadership, exploring the corridors of the labyrinth and encouraging others to follow them toward a better future becomes a call that leaders want to answer, even, and especially, when it is hard.

The Acceleration of the Unknown for Leaders in the Twenty-First Century

Leadership is hard. It has become especially so in the twenty-first century. Never has there been a time where change has been so rapid, unpredictable, and unknowable. We live in times of great ambiguity, more so than ever before, where the digital, hyper-connected global arena in which we work can be overwhelming.

Knowing all that is relevant to our business life and how to stay ahead of it is impossible. With the emergence of the Internet, business life changed dramatically. What used to be seen as far away and irrelevant now can have a direct impact on your ability to compete for customers, talent, and reputation. In this context, never has the job of a leader been tougher to fulfill, and never have we needed leadership more, at all levels, in all walks of life.

The world is awash with news about leaders and a dire need for good ones. Much disappointment is expressed about leaders from those in government and big corporations to small businesses and community groups. To be sure, leaders have fallen short many times, taking safe, known routes while avoiding the realities of their situations and the risks of change. Given the pressure on executives from boards and investors to produce robust top and bottom lines, the temptation to make safe, experience-tested business moves is high. That works, until the market changes, as it inevitably does, and does so more quickly than ever before. The result is that the same old, same old no longer supports sustainable profitability.

The failure of same old, same old was quite evident in the Great Recession of 2007 to 2009. During that crisis, many executives disappeared behind closed doors into the solitude of their offices or literally into the woods where they could hide from their bewilderment at what all the bad economic news really meant. Even those who had been through four or five recessions in their careers, enough to know the patterns, knew that this one had no form file. No one knew how to understand, much less solve this recession.

With the world so in flux, executives, rather than risking new approaches, fled from them. Companies put in place a new business development plan, often asking their employees to become salespeople, including career introverts who could barely manage a social conversation, much less a sale of goods or services. Websites were redone with clever new phrases without new strategies that reflected the changing reality. Not surprisingly, the numbers failed to improve. Employees quietly gathered at the door, waiting for the economic gates to lift, freeing them to go elsewhere.

At the same time, when leaders pay attention to market evolution and take on the risks to advance new ideas, the avalanche of criticism about something new that so often erupts can be discouraging. The leaders who used the Great Recession to scrutinize the emerging market came out of that era ahead of their competitors. Successful companies, such as Netflix movie rentals and Groupon daily deals, emerged during this period to answer a consumer desire for affordable entertainment. Revenue for Keurig, single-cup coffee makers (made then by Green Mountain Coffee Roasters, now known as Keurig Green Mountain) increased 86 percent during the recession, according to Capital IQ, as consumers looked for a way to have a Starbucks quality cup of coffee in their homes and offices at prices lower than what they would have paid at a Starbucks store.

How the Unknown Shows Up in the Daily Life of a Leader

If you read the literature on executive presence, one of the first adjectives used to describe a successful executive is "confident," often followed by "self-assured." It suggests that only by being on top of their facts, interpretations, and predicted outcomes will leaders inspire others to follow them. With the world changing each second of the day, how is that possible?

Things we do not know surround us. That is, when we pay attention. Yet too often we do not, and our lack of awareness will prevent leaders from starting down the pathway toward bigger bets. Competitors can come out with a compelling product when we assumed they lacked the capability to create it. Our favorite executive can leave to join a startup firm having tired of not having enough authority to act. Our customers can decide lower prices mean more than their loyalty to our brand.

The unknown shows up in many ways that we might not even recognize. Not knowing is that empty space where the answer is not immediately in front of you. It is that pause in the conversation you cannot instantly fill with anything that feels like a real answer. It is a moment where you are not sure where to go next. It is a yawning cavern of silence where all you might hear is self-doubt or skepticism. It is a sleepless night where you can only imagine bad outcomes.

The unknown appears in virtually every aspect of daily organizational life. It appears when you are:

- Releasing a product intended to serve a need not yet addressed.

- Going to meet a potential client with whom you have never dealt and until your visit would have never thought of you as a possible service provider.

- Restructuring an executive team in a way that aligns responsibilities with new strategies and new champions.

- Holding a conversation with a valued direct report to tell her that you cannot give her a highly prized promotion, but nevertheless you need her to stay with the company and remain motivated.

- Entering into a conversation with another executive, who for some reason scares you and whose opinion deeply matters to you.

- Telling a business partner that his favorite vendor, whom he has known since college days, has fallen short again, costing your company significant money and reputation.

The list goes on. In fact, the examples are legion if we are willing to push further, stretch wider, and move higher to try to make things better. In none of these instances do we know the outcome. We know only where to start, maybe a couple of turns along the way, a general notion of how we would like to end up, and no guarantee that we will arrive at the point we wanted to reach.

The Two Sources of the Unknown

The unknown shows up in two different and equally important ways: the external unknown and the internal unknown.

The External Unknown

The external unknown is what we do not know about the environment in which we work. It includes everything from the global economy to our leadership team culture. We have to deal with the world the way it is, not as we would like it to be. To see what is happening around us without varnish is essential to generating relevant ideas that address the future of our organizations.

Business consultant Jim Collins referred to this idea in *Good to Great: Why Some Companies Make the Leap . . . and Others Don't* as confronting the "brutal facts of reality." Brutal facts can be painful and feel well worth avoiding. They can confuse our business plans and disrupt strategies.

Here are some examples:

- Admitting that our sales have grown primarily as a result of aggressive discounted pricing rather than the allure of owning an edgy new product design.

- Not understanding that our clients have come to prefer integrated design services rather than the stand-alone premier quality specialty services provided by our firm can hurt not only the bottom line but also the pride of our expert professionals who can suffer loss of work and reputation as a consequence.

- Having a fantastic company work culture is great, but if our company cannot provide the robust pay and benefits packages offered by a new well-funded competitor down the street, attracting top talent will be far more difficult than it already is.

Hard as the external reality can appear, only by facing it directly to understand its underpinnings can a leader discover the opportunities. A famous example comes from World War II when British Prime Minister Winston Churchill grew frustrated with the information coming from his cabinet ministers, members of Parliament, and senior military officers whom he perceived as slanting vital information to fit political agendas rather than actual facts. To get around them, Churchill formed the Statistical Office to gather data on labor, tank strength, daily production, and technical developments. It allowed Churchill to make shrewd strategic decisions based on the "cold-blooded facts."

Conversely, Jim Balsillie, co-CEO of Research in Motion (RIM), maker of the BlackBerry phone, balked at the rise of a smartphone that offered functions that went way beyond telephone and email service, starting with Internet search, quickly followed by restaurant reservation tools, online news services, and the exploding world of social media. In fact, in 2008, he said in an interview, when asked about the future of BlackBerry and the potential competition with iPhone, "I don't sorta look up too much, I don't look down too much . . . The great fun is doing what you do every day. I'm sort of a poster child for not doing anything but what we do every day." When asked directly about what he thought about the iPhone as competition, Balsillie uttered these prophetic words with a dismissive chuckle, "I don't really think about it . . . We're a very poorly diversified portfolio." (See "Interview with BlackBerry co-CEO Jim Balsillie," April 1, 2008, CBC, *The Hour.*) His reward for ignoring the rising interest in the smartphone as a source of entertainment and social connectivity was seeing an 87 percent drop in the RIM stock price between 2010 and 2013 due in large part to the rise of iPhone.

The Internal Unknown

The internal unknown is what we do not know about ourselves. Not knowing ourselves can prevent us from engaging with our own internal reality where great ideas are born and with the people we need to help us with those ideas.

To see clearly the world outside requires us to see clearly what is inside of us. Self-awareness is power. It surfaces who we uniquely are, what values we hold dear, and the dreams we want to realize. We will never know everything about ourselves. However, our openness to see ourselves as we are, not as we should be, inspires trust in others. It allows them to connect to us and to our dreams for making things better. That connection produces the strategic ideas we need to build the future of our organizations.

Not knowing ourselves can be a major barrier to success. As nineteenth-century Russian writer Leo Tolstoy wisely observed, "A man is like a fraction whose numerator is what he is and whose denominator is what he thinks of himself. The larger the denominator, the smaller the fraction." In other words, if we think we are something we are not, the channels to new ideas and the involvement of others becomes clogged.

The Impact of Our Life Stories: We all travel with our unique life stories that steer us, whether we like them or not. While we have been given many gifts that inspire us to lead, we also live with lessons from the past that can be painful, particularly if not used as a learning opportunity. The more we are able to uncover and acknowledge the influences of the past, the easier it is to see the future without obstructing filters.

Below are some examples:

- Coming out of a hyper-competitive, toxic work environment that discouraged taking intellectual risks for fear of ridicule should not condemn us to pursue only safe, conventional ideas.

- Understanding how a parent's perfectionism affected our self-view is an important step toward not placing a perfectionist burden on ourselves.

- Detaching ourselves from the impact of a bullying older sibling who made us shy away from conflict in our adult life will help us to find our voices to speak up when we need to do so.

Uncovering and decoding the past takes work. Yet when we avoid such discovery, we limit our ability to stretch into the unknown and take the kind of risks that will bring about positive change.

Knowing more about ourselves does not mean we can eliminate the past. *We cannot change our life stories, but we can change how we behave as a result of them.*

Separating the clogging effect of one's past from the reality of the present will help see the way to new possibilities for the future of one's organization.

What Is the Journey of Not Knowing?

The Journey of Not Knowing is the pathway leaders must take through the unknown to pursue bigger bets for their organizations. To do that, we need to be *comfortable with the discomfort of not knowing.*

In organizational life, the unknown means not knowing how the bigger bet will be received, if we can win the buy-in and resources to pull it off, or whether it will work at all. It also means not knowing the complexity of the human dynamics that make up any organization, including our own psychological wiring. Political agendas, individual histories, and blind spots can prevent even the most compelling ideas from going forward. How leaders face those challenges can make all the difference to the success of their bigger bets.

By its nature, the Journey of Not Knowing surfaces feelings of discomfort. Discomfort, whether it comes in the form of mild anxiety, medium-level worry, or outright panic, is an inevitable consequence to going into the unknown. Where outcomes are not known, risks take over. They show up in such questions as

- Will they laugh at me for suggesting this idea?
- Will it work?
- Will it cost me my reputation?
- Will I lose my job as a result of this idea?
- Who might try to stand in the way of this, and why?
- What happens if it fails and nobody trusts me again?

These might seem like "unadult" feelings that our rational selves say we should surmount. At the same time, they are real, and they are particularly real to a leader whose job is to build the enterprise and make a difference.

To navigate the labyrinth, a leader has to face the discomfort caused by the unknown. This means overcoming the many defensive behaviors that can rise up in front of us giving short-term comfort but taking us off the pathway to the larger strategic ideas that lie beyond. As described in greater detail in the next pages and in Part 4, these defensive behaviors, called "hooks," include such ubiquitous things as micromanagement and conflict avoidance. They will prevent a leader from delivering on his or her role.

The Journey of Not Knowing helps leaders to recognize their hooks and find a strategy to unhook from them with the fuel of "drivers." Drivers provide purpose, long or short term, for pursuing bigger bets. While they do not remove the fear the world of new ideas can cause, they give leaders a reason to push forward toward the future.

Hooks

The labyrinth to the bigger bets contains a minefield of hooks. Hooks are defensive behaviors that can buffer the scariness of new or unexpected outcomes, but prevent us from moving forward toward our bigger bets. Defensive behaviors in themselves are not necessarily bad. Defensives protect us from pain, allowing us to function in a world that is not always fair or happy. They give us the ability to work around difficult situations and pull from them the best we can when much is out of our control.

People bring a diversity of behavior to work. Ideally, most of it is productive. In reality, everyone has moments of less-than-ideal behavior. We can fall into counterproductive actions that relieve our tension but do not cure the problem. When confronted with a particularly challenging project, it sometimes feels better to fiddle with setting up the file folders or choosing the font for the presentation rather than diving into the core issue that makes the assignment hard.

Defensive behaviors become hooks when they create a barrier to our success. If we are momentarily bored, playing with the layout of the presentation boards serves as a nice diversion. If, however, we find ourselves fooling around with the layout, fonts, and other items that are in the purview of others, or, even more significantly, as a way to avoid dealing with the questionable strategy behind that presentation, then we are "hooked."

Hooks come in many forms and are familiar if not by name, by characteristics to anyone who has spent time in the work world. They include such behaviors as micromanagement, perfectionism, and conflict avoidance.

Hooks can yield the following results:

- Give us instant feedback to quell the anxiety of not knowing the bigger result.

- Help us feel like we have things under control even when we do not.

- Remove us from adversarial situations when we do not know how others will react.

- Allow us to ignore how much the others in our organization pay attention to us and depend on what we do.

Reading through this list, you might well ask, what is wrong with any of this? The answer is "nothing," if the behavior allows you to accomplish your leadership goals. When hooks become a problem is when they prevent us from thinking in a broader, more strategic way or receiving the best work from people on whose talent we depend to achieve our bigger bets.

Many hooks exist. The ten most common hooks are listed below and further described in Part 4.

The ten hooks are

- micromanagement
- perfectionism
- conflict avoidance
- codependence
- taking the credit
- personalizing
- failure to delegate
- disengagement
- poor boundaries
- inauthenticity

Most of these hooks catch everyone at least some of the time. It is a normal byproduct of being human. We encounter different hooks at different times. An adversarial colleague might trigger conflict avoidance in us on a day we are feeling confused or troubled. On another day when we are feeling strong, centered, and clear about an issue, we might be able to deal quite effectively with any conflict caused by that person. The variability can trip up our progress as leaders when we need to achieve something important with that colleague and it coincides with a day when we are not feeling strong, centered, or clear.

There also can be more than one active hook in a given situation. For example, we can withdraw from an uncomfortable interaction, both disengaging ourselves from its emotional charge and avoiding conflict. We can slip into a perfectionist mode and impose that perfectionism on our team in a micromanaging way when we feel out of control and worried about accountability for the results.

At the foundation of each hook lies a reaction to the discomfort of dealing with the risks of the unknown. The cost is losing the promise of the possibilities that lie beyond.

Drivers

Being comfortable with the discomfort of not knowing does not mean a leader has to struggle painfully through the labyrinth of uncertainty with no reward. A leader needs a reason to make that journey: something that will provide navigation lights to guide the way through those twists and turns. These navigation lights are called "drivers."

Drivers provide a person with direction, a higher purpose as to why he or she wants to do something and go through dark corridors to reach the exit where the new idea comes into being.

Drivers generate fuel to plow through discomfort. They make it possible to face and overcome the perceived impossibilities.

Finding a "driver" helps "unhook" a leader's hooks. They can fit a specific situation such as a competitive feeling with an industry peer. They also can emanate from a deeper place, born out of personal history and values. The key is they give leaders a reason to overcome adversity and deliver on bigger bets.

Drivers appear in two forms: situational drivers and core drivers.

Situational drivers provide motivation for dealing with tough situations because the cost of not dealing is worse. Deciding that there is no way you want a certain competitor to beat you by winning a proposal can provide you with motivation to tolerate the anxiety of working with your ruthless and unpredictable business strategy team whose analytical talent you need to beat the competition.

More powerful are core drivers, fundamental facts of personal history, values, and psychology that make people who they are. Core drivers often come from early life, derived from family dynamics or life experiences outside the family in the work world and other environments. A driver can come from overbearing parents who do not want us to achieve more than they did in the world, a death in the family that leads us to want to achieve something in honor of that person's memory, or a cherished friend who inspires us by his or her own life and a strong belief in our ability to do the same. The Arrow story includes many examples of how critical events and people influence individuals and how those influences propel them ultimately in a positive direction.

The more core the driver, the more fuel it gives us to weave through the labyrinth of uncertainty. Drivers can vary by context. However, the more we draw on what we learn about our life histories, values, and dreams, the more energy we will have to achieve our bigger bets.

Why Bother Taking the Journey?

What can get lost in the conversation about the scariness of undefined odds against success is the enormous opportunity that comes with the role of a leader. Leaders must navigate the unknown to succeed. While the journey through the unknown is chock full of risks that inevitably come with new ideas, the reward for taking such a journey is the enormous satisfaction of seeing new ideas become real, making lives healthier, more productive, and satisfying.

At Amazon in 1999, we prevailed over the many potential impossibilities in Germany, and my team got another nanosecond to celebrate. In the larger picture, that was a lot. It was important to them as a team and to me as a leader to have triumphed over adversity and threaded our way through the many dark corridors of the labyrinth. Was it scary? Definitely, but that was the only way we could find a successful exit.

Navigating the discomfort of not knowing to achieve something better feeds the hunger of leaders to make an impact. Sometimes it even leads to someone saying to you, "Thank you. You really made a difference."

Part 3

ARROW, INC.: ONE DAY IN MARCH

Arrow, Inc.

THE STORY THAT follows describes one business day at Arrow, Inc. On that day Arrow has to meet a tight deadline to win a large new project that represents a bigger bet critical to its future.

Searching for the truth leads the eight members of the Arrow leadership team to confront the unknowns in their business environment and themselves. To do that, all of them have to embark on the Journey of Not Knowing. Each avoids the unknown by hiding in one or more hooks. With the help of others, private self-reflection, and triggering events, they find personal drivers to overcome the discomfort of what they need to learn about themselves and the situation to remove the threat to the company's bigger bet.

The narrative contains other characters, including leaders from outside Arrow. While their stories are not told with equal depth, they represent familiar forces in the work world. We cannot have the world as we want it to be, but must see it for what it is, regardless of the obstacles it presents. As leaders we must understand and learn to work with what we can and cannot know about the behavior of others.

While Arrow, Inc., is a fictional company, its plot and characters arise from an amalgam of real-world experiences. No one character is someone I know. However, the behaviors and personal histories flow from people I have met throughout the years. For what I learned from them, I am most grateful.

This story takes place during the course of one day. While the transformations experienced by the leadership team members during this day might be accelerated for the sake of condensing the plot, personal breakthroughs often occur in times of crisis. That assumes, of course, that the leaders are able to come to grips with the unknown.

Cast of Characters

Arrow, Inc., Leadership Team
>Barry Sanford, chief executive officer, founder, Arrow, Inc.
>Claudia Milgram, chief financial officer, Finance
>Janelle Wilbert, general counsel, Legal
>Simon Majeski, vice president, Engineering
>Nigel Johnson, vice president, Sales
>Marco Perez, vice president, Operations
>Arnie Butler, assistant vice president, Sales
>Janey Fahey, director, Marketing

Other Arrow People
>Marjorie Perault, executive assistant to Barry Sanford
>Ray Hillman, manager, Facilities
>Michael Marcourt, team member, Marketing
>Joyce Levinson, assistant, Legal
>Alecia Perelli, receptionist
>Charles Kramer, chair, Arrow board of directors
>Bill Morely, outside legal counsel

People from Outside Arrow
>Cathryn Porter, chief executive officer, founder, Porter, Inc.
>Mark Miller, chief executive officer, Zinc, Inc.
>Miriam Fallow, executive assistant to Cathryn Porter
>Senil Kapoor, engineer, Porter, Inc.
>Bernard Wu, engineer

The Arrow Team

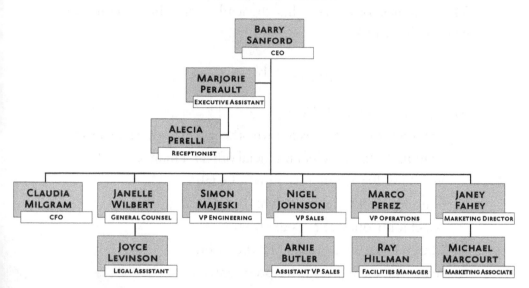

Prologue
The Journey Begins: Arrow Inc., Early January

The ultra-modern conference room reeked of cheap takeout food and the nervous sweat of eight unhappy people. It was after hours, quiet, and dark outside. Inside, the Arrow, Inc., leadership team sat in silence, each person dealing privately with the obvious tension in the room.

Nigel Johnson, vice president of Sales, drummed his fingers on the lid of his laptop and kept glancing at Claudia Milgram, the company CFO. She ignored him. Instead she looked down and slowly turned the pages of the financial report she had presented to the group. Next to her sat Janelle Wilbert, the general counsel, perched ramrod straight on her chair, clicking her ballpoint pen as if in a trance.

Across the table Marco Perez, vice president of Operations, smiled nervously and clasped his hands neatly in front of him. Janey Fahey, Marketing director, sat by Marco and tapped distractedly on her smartphone without so much as a glance at the screen. Nigel's second in command, Arnie Butler, peeked down the table at his usually garrulous boss, waiting for him to say something . . . anything. Still, nobody spoke.

Slumped in a chair nearest the door, Simon Majeski, vice president of Engineering, fixed his attention on the remaining corner of a fully loaded pulled pork sandwich held fast between his thumb and forefinger. After two or three seconds of study, he leaned back slowly and shoved the triangle into his mouth, wiping a trickle of juice off his cheek with exaggerated delicacy. Loud chewing filled the room, followed by louder crumpling, then a whizzing noise as a brown bag flew into the vicinity of a corner wastebasket.

Barry Sanford, the company CEO, sat at the head of the table and watched the bag sail to the corner of the room. It beat looking at his team. When the bag hit the floor, as if on cue, his eyes moved back to the group.

Clearing his throat, he began, "Well, I guess there is nothing more to discuss here. We are no longer on the Zinc project and have lost the critical strategic positioning that project would have given us. We have yet to hear an explanation, and I suspect that none is forthcoming. That leaves us with no choice but to move on to something new."

He hesitated briefly, waiting for a reaction. When none came, he resumed, "While we are doing that, we have to keep the rest of our business going. So, ladies and gentlemen, if there is nothing more to add, let us adjourn and go tend to the enterprise."

Laptops snapped shut. Papers slid into folders. Chairs rolled back. The room quickly emptied, except for Barry who remained seated alone.

His eyes fixated on the grain of the conference room table as he sat deep in thought. *What happened? We were doing such great work for those people. Then, poof! It was gone, with nothing more than a cryptic, "we have decided to discontinue this project," followed by radio silence. Why?* He did not know even where to begin to figure it out. He squeezed his eyes shut for a moment, then he rose to leave.

Little did he realize that two months later a chance to find out what happened would come his way.

Chapter 1: One Day in March, Early Morning—The Dance around the Unknown

In the business world we have a love affair with knowing things, all sorts of things. Success in business is equated with the right moves, smart ones that suggest that the mover actually could see ahead of others, predict something they did not understand or assume what people intended without having to ask them. In fact, thinking that we know for sure what is going to work and what people really believe is an illusion. That illusion keeps us from recognizing the importance of what we do not know and what we need to learn to move things into the future.

Barry

Barry Sanford hiked his gym bag over his shoulder and took one last look at himself in the mirror. He raked his fingers through his still dark brown hair, arranging it into a tasteful cross between studied casual and captain of industry. He patted a stray piece back into place, smiled at the effect, and turned toward the door. Heading to the exit of the health club, he waved goodbye to his trainer and stepped into the early morning light.

He strode down the sidewalk lined with new planters containing skinny trees and small pompom-shaped shrubs, the city planners' vision for gentrifying the former light manufacturing part of town. Three blocks later Barry arrived at the four-story brick office building that housed his ten-year-old company. The newly renovated building sat in the rediscovered cool part of the city packed with venture-backed startups and their alumni. The street pulsed with the intensity of business experiments. Barry loved its catalytic energy.

He walked across the wide lobby, stepping without thinking around the crack in the terracotta tile, a souvenir of a piece of camera equipment dropped before a new product release press conference.

"Good morning, Mr. Sanford!" Alecia Perelli, the Arrow receptionist, prided herself on setting a positive tone for all people entering the company, including its CEO.

"Good morning, Alecia." Barry said and popped into the elevator that took him to the fourth floor. He walked briskly down the ochre corridor that led to his corner office suite. He continued past the outer office desk occupied by Marjorie Perault, his imperious and indispensable assistant. He turned his head briefly in her direction, called out, "Morning!" and crossed the threshold into his office.

Marjorie did not bother looking up, at least in any way that was obvious. She busied herself arranging her snacks and reading material for the day. A medium-height, square-built woman of a certain age, she favored a no-nonsense neutral color dress (today it was dark gray), medium-height pumps, and a beaded chain, attached to her glasses, dangling around her neck. All this was topped by carefully colored hair wound into an updo held tightly in place by industrial strength hair products. When she bothered to look up, she would peer over her readers in a way that there was no doubt as to who was in charge.

This morning, as on all mornings, Marjorie surveyed Barry as he motored by, assessing his pace, facial expression, and mood.

Aside from the impact of each on her quality of life that day, sitting always open on her computer was the novel in the making. It broke up the boredom of years spent carrying out the agendas, smart or misguided, of various senior executives. If anyone at Arrow knew about the novel, no one, including Barry, had the nerve to say anything for fear they would later end up in it. It was true she regarded anything that traveled past her desk as fair game for literary material. Today, Barry's entry offered no interesting leads, but the day was young.

Having ducked Marjorie's scrutiny this morning, or so he thought, Barry entered the sanctuary of his office and went straight to his desk. Before him waited a desktop of random things, some more random than others. For reasons long lost to time, he organized the surface of his desk by quadrant. The upper left quadrant held industry magazines, research papers, charity auction invitations, circulars, and several internal announcements that obviously had ignored the "paperless" policy.

In the upper right quadrant of the desk lay internal reports, memos, and a curled copy of last year's strategic plan. To his left in the lower quadrant were various internal proposals for training and recruiting, personal bills from his trainer and his favorite men's clothing store that kept him in trendy attire befitting a tech executive, a wrapper from yesterday's lunch (or was it the day before?), and a couple of contracts he was supposed to sign once he got around to reading them. There also was a pile of reports from the Excelsior project, a personal favorite of his in which he took a great proprietary interest.

In the lower right corner sat one thing, and that item was the most recent company financial report. His highly controlling

CFO refused to send out digital copies of her reports until the relevant parties had viewed them to make sure no compromising figures floated into the digital domain. He sighed and slowly lifted its front page. At the bottom appeared a number he did not expect to see, and it was not a good number.

As he stared at the page, Marjorie wandered in with a couple of trade magazines draped over her right arm.

"Which quadrant for these latest additions?"

"Lower left."

His flat tone caught Marjorie's attention. "Something wrong?"

"Yeah, this number, but I don't know why. I haven't seen results like this since our holy war with social media."

"Uh-oh. I'll leave you alone to climb back into that foxhole. Holler if you need anything else." She dropped the trade magazines into the lower left quadrant and returned to her desk.

A Brief History of Arrow and Its Encounter with Social Media

Barry continued to chew on the financial report. Then his mind wandered back to better days.

Until ten months ago, life at Arrow, Inc., had been sweet. Barry founded the company in 2005 and was its first, and so far only, chief executive officer. The company provided software productivity tools for the business community. The more businesspeople moved around throughout the day, the more they relied on their computers to carry the bulk of their business day.

With vastly increased storage capacity on portable computers, businesspeople moved the bulk of their vital information from paper files onto their electronic devices. With more information being packed into a small space came a greater need to organize that information. Arrow supported that space with its first signature product, Sizzle, a file-organizing software product that recognized keywords and recommended folders to stow information.

Barry loved the tempo of the business world, its quick pace, changeability, and demand for better things. He also loved, his desktop notwithstanding, finding ways to provide order to it that would free up workers' energy for creative work, rather than putting a lot of time and thought into finding where they had housed that work. Developing fast, efficient, and intuitive organizing tools for documents and files seemed made to order for that challenge.

Arrow had evolved with its market, developing a mobile version of its product, as more of its customers used smartphones and tablets in lieu of computers. Life continued to be good with an average annual sales increase of 15 percent. The company, privately held by a dozen prominent local businesspeople, received favorable press and pleased its investors.

That is, until the advent of social media, which did not try to organize business information. It did talk about those who did. One of the organizers that social media discussed was Arrow.

Arrow had had its challenges throughout the years. Its sales-people made promises to its customers for integrated tools, only to find out that Engineering had not yet produced a critical feature. Engineering burned the midnight oil to address a feature that customers universally demanded, only to find out that Operations could not roll it out due to a distraction with a major vendor dispute. Such was the life of a technology firm. It was annoying, but it did not slow the overall pace of growth.

That changed with the rollout of Sizzle 2.0, a major upgrade from the original organizing product. Sizzle 2.0 promised a wide variety of new features, including suggestions for those who did not love to organize but loved having devices that did. Due to an error in the product development process, files that did not fit any particular category automatically went to "Trash," leaving the owner of the information with a lost file. Arrow customers let out a major uproar, demanding a return of their money and moving to competitors who had less robust offerings that did not come with the baggage of the software glitch.

Many refunds, apologetic emails, and handholding sessions later, the "Trash" debacle moved behind Arrow. The good life resumed, at least so Barry thought, until he peered at his financial report this morning.

"So what is going on with the drop in this month's profit?" mumbled Barry. He leaned forward to parse the numbers.

Arnie and the Threat to the Bigger Bet

As Barry settled into his analysis, Arnie Butler, the up-and-coming number two sales executive, burst through the door. While he was dressed in traditional sales-guy khaki pants and an expensive white shirt, he nevertheless appeared disheveled. His carefully cut hair that usually lay in tasteful waves had a spikey bit shooting off the left side, looking like he had been trying to yank it out.

Barry calmly took this in. *No use in getting excited until I know I need to,* he thought to himself. Then Arnie began.

"We just heard back from Cathryn Porter's firm. Good news! They are seriously interested in our proposal." Cathryn Porter's firm, with the catchy name, Porter, Inc., produced various consumer-friendly organizing tools including a calendar app that had been well received by the consumer market. Porter, Inc., wanted to link the calendar to the files of materials important to the user and expand the platform. Arrow had proposed to develop a program that would do that.

Barry, sensing that this news alone would not lead to hair pulling, decided to move the conversation quickly to the relevant point. "And the not-so-good news?"

"Well, they want answers to five additional questions, and they have to have a response before their board meeting tonight. Kind of tight I'd say."

Barry shifted into his concerned but even-tempered executive mode. "That depends on the five questions."

"Oh, they're not too terrible." Arnie struggled to recover his cool. "They want to know things like our cost per developer on our most recent projects, which is a little tricky since our developers hate to record time, and we don't yet have good data on that stuff. Our friend Simon over in Engineering said—"

"I don't care what our friend Simon said. What else?"

"They also want to know our target profit margin for projects, our actual versus budget details on three of our most recent projects, and our position on who will own the intellectual property when we are done."

"Wow, nosy bunch over there. We can come up with something. What's the fifth thing?"

Arnie, surprised that Barry had been counting, hesitated.

"Well?"

"Well . . ." Arnie started slowly, then catching Barry's darkening expression, picked up the tempo. "They want to know why Zinc fired us."

Up until this minute, Barry had been only half listening. This last comment caught his full attention.

"Huh? What's that got to do with anything? What business is that of theirs? And, for the record, we were NOT fired! We quit working for them because there was no way we could win with them. They took forever to tell us their program requirements, couldn't answer our most basic questions, and when they finally did, we'd get some gibberish that didn't sound like English. Speaking of English, where's Nigel?" Nigel was the vice president of Sales. British, forever on the move, and socially facile, he cut an energetic form. That is, when he was around.

Suddenly aware of how reactive he sounded, Barry paused, drew a deep breath, and spoke again, this time adopting the more contained, modulated tone he had been practicing with his executive coach. "Besides, there's no way we can share that. The details of a client relationship are confidential, whether it's a current client or not."

He snapped his mouth shut, working hard to sustain his equanimity. It didn't work. Something tugged him from underneath.

"WHAT kind of asinine question is that? Who ARE these Porter people? I have done everything to earn their trust. I have listened, answered honestly, and given them a major chunk of my precious time doing so. And this is my reward?"

He grabbed his water bottle from the lower right quadrant and polished off its contents in three big gulps. He plunked the empty bottle down on his desk and glowered at Arnie.

Arnie stared down at the dark gray carpet not knowing how to respond, other than to say in a small voice that Nigel was out on the road somewhere seeing customers. He then returned to tugging at his hair.

Claudia Hits and Runs

While Arnie studied the carpet, in glided Claudia Milgram, the company's ever-efficient, smug, and politically toxic CFO.

"Weeelll, gentlemen. You two don't look particularly happy with life this morning. What seems to be the problem?" Her voice dripped with insincerity.

Barry thought he would rather die than share anything with the self-serving and calculating Claudia. Tall and always stylishly dressed, she required the attention of any room she entered. She knew her stuff, at least when it came to finance, and that was useful. He also believed that when push came to even a tiny shove, she would happily land him in front of a train if the board of directors was riding in it. She was particularly chummy with its chairperson. Her relationship with him trumped all other considerations as far as she, and the rest of the company, was concerned.

"Nothing, Claudia. The usual client nonsense. No reason for concern . . . yet."

"Yet . . ." Claudia gave Barry a satisfied smile. She loved pushing Barry into vulnerable corners. "And what exactly do we mean by 'yet'?"

"I mean 'nothing' until I say it is 'something.'"

"Oooohhhh . . ." She said, feigning fear, and slid out the door.

"Hate that woman," Barry hissed under his breath.

Fortunately, Arnie hadn't heard Barry. He was busy swimming through random thoughts of what to do about Porter. Arrow desperately needed the Porter business. Porter represented a high level of status in the mobile productivity tools app sector. It produced easy-to-use, reliable products with an attractive user interface. It had a major reputation for having its finger firmly on the pulse of the consumer market of mobile device users.

Porter also had a reputation as a great place to work. Somehow through the power of social media, the "Trash" story, old as it was, had been institutionalized in the social media airwaves. Arrow found itself facing a challenge to its reputation, something that was totally new to its leaders. They had only created a Facebook page last year.

Arrow started out having a positive market brand, but as each year went by, it looked more and more like yesterday's news. A deal with Porter would be a major endorsement. Knowing that, the Porter people prided themselves by being particularly tough and picky about whom they chose to work with. They viewed each alliance as not merely a vendor relationship, but as an extension of their corporate identity. Despite all efforts to the contrary, word had gotten out that Arrow was wooing their business. Not winning it was worse than not having tried at all, and definitely a blow to the Arrow image.

While Barry was all too keenly aware of the extreme importance of winning the Porter deal, he was not ruminating on that right now. He directed his thoughts to how he could make Claudia's life as miserable as she made his. So far, he was not making much progress.

At this point, Arnie was looking at Barry. Barry was looking out the window, his thoughts drifting to another place as he wondered, *There must be a better way to earn a living.*

Barry Peers at the Unknown, Then Reverses Course

Leadership asks you to enter unmapped territory and find the best of you. To lead, you have to see without filters, engage in what is real, and move others forward. In other words, leadership is not easy, and a lot of time and energy can be directed at running away from the reality that provides vital clues to the future.

Barry continued to stare out the window while Arnie fidgeted behind him. He wondered how he had missed noticing that the trees next to the parking lot were finally budding. He recognized that even having a parking lot, especially one with a row of old trees next to it, was a rarity in the fast-growing metropolitan area. Arrow had managed to find its building on a site at the edge of the expanding urban revitalization footprint that sprawled out from the modern high-rise buildings of the city center. Barry knew that it was only a matter of time before the parking lot would become either a multistory parking structure or a modern office building with historic building design pretensions.

I guess it's time to give the car its spring wash and repair that ding in the side where my son decided to use the car as a bike rack, Barry thought. *Oh, why even bother? I hate that piece of junk. Maybe I'll take Ellie out this weekend to shop for a new car. Only this morning she was complaining that all her friends with sleek hybrids were now upgrading to electric cars. We, of course, have an antediluvian gas-guzzler.*

Barry favored a modern image, except when it came to cars. His father, a well-regarded bank executive, equated a late-model car with business success. When Barry was growing up, every Saturday morning he and his brother had to wash and polish his dad's latest wheels. Barry did not mind physical labor. He did mind washing and polishing his dad's car, especially because after he had finished, his dad would disappear to the golf course for the rest of the day.

As an adult, Barry despised new cars. Unfortunately, Ellie was not of the same mind...

Didn't I have something else I had to do this weekend? Better check my calendar. He picked up the cell phone on his desk.

As he peered down at his calendar, out of the corner of his eye he caught the nervous expression on Arnie's face and the tuft of hair still sticking up on his head. Seeing that tuft brought Barry out of his reverie.

As if there had been no break in the conversation, Barry resumed, "Where were we?"

"We were trying to figure out how to answer Porter's questions."

"Oh, yeah. Go talk to Simon. He can give you the hourly metrics. He might be awful at making his engineers keep time, but he has been around the block enough times to know how long it takes to do things."

Simon Majeski was the brilliant Arrow vice president of Engineering. He had been at Arrow since it opened, weathered multiple storms, and somehow emerged from them unscathed. How he managed to do that was a mystery to many. Simon did what he pleased most of the time, leaving social niceties to others.

Arnie shuddered at the thought of descending into the smelly, murky den that was Simon's office. As he was deciding which hazmat suit to wear to go there, Barry interrupted his inner flow of thoughts.

"Ask Marco about the project margins. It will spare you a trip to Claudia," he said with a sly smile. Marco was the conscientious vice president of Operations who derived great pride from his meticulous, well-thought-out systems. His group provided project management oversight to all internal initiatives and account management to large Arrow customers. For some reason, he also was one of the few people in the company Claudia did not revel in thwarting. She seemed to derive job satisfaction giving the runaround to other conscientious people. No one understood why she treated Marco differently. Whatever the reason, it allowed Marco to collect standard financial information from Finance, so long as it required no extra effort on the part of anyone.

Arnie smiled back, "What about the IP?"

"Go see the legal dragons," Barry let out a pleased cackle. "I'm sure Janelle will be happy to set you straight." Janelle Wilbert, Arrow general counsel, and Barry only occasionally saw eye to eye. An arch debater, she loved to remind Barry of his analytical limitations. She managed the legal affairs of the company with an air of serious authority, making sure her group worked efficiently and to a high standard. Even birthday parties were held on time, each with a perfectly decorated cake at the center of the law department document production table that would be cleared for the occasion.

She was not without flexibility, that is, so long as she had the final word . . . and she got to her exercise class punctually at noon on Mondays, Wednesdays, and Fridays, or whenever else she deemed appropriate.

"Sure . . ." responded Arnie and started to turn toward the door. Then he remembered. "Wait, what about Zinc?"

"What about Zinc? It's none of Porter's business," Barry stretched his back against his chair and swiveled around to his computer screen.

Arnie took his cue and zoomed out the door. Marjorie watched his departure with studied interest. She could smell some good material emerging there.

Back in his office, Barry stared abstractly at his screen for a few moments, his mood dark. *Zinc . . . what was that about? Those people were so difficult. But then again, so was Arrow from time to time. But, the questions and requirements those Zinc techs had! They kept demanding weird features I couldn't imagine anyone wanting.*

He groaned and redirected his attention to the lower left quadrant of the desk where the Excelsior pile beamed back at him.

Excelsior was a new project he championed, after the fall of Zinc, to customize the latest version of the Sizzle product for the legal profession. He had been thinking about it for several months, but until Zinc gave its notice Barry had not felt a sufficient sense of urgency to do anything about it. Now things looked differently. He smiled as if seeing an old friend and pulled the pile toward him.

Barry Backs Out of the Labyrinth

In their quest to scratch the itch of discovery, leaders will stick their heads into the labyrinth and venture down its first corridor. Then the corridor abruptly turns. Ahead lies darkness, still and quiet. How tempting it is to turn on your heel and retrace your steps to the light behind you, the place where you have already been.

With Arnie cleared out of his office, Barry dug with gusto into the Excelsior files. After the failure of the Zinc project, Barry felt nervous and adrift. He spent many nights churning around in his bed trying to understand what had happened with that project. No one on his leadership team could provide any insight as to where things went off the rails, other than how difficult Zinc was as a client. In the end, Barry decided that Zinc was one of those clients that was too dysfunctional to achieve any meaningful results. It was a relief that the deal died. Now to have it resurface as a critical factor in the Porter deal was beyond inconvenient.

What Barry also concluded was that without the Zinc deal, Arrow had lost an entry into a more technologically sophisticated customer base than what it presently served. Sizzle gave ordinary, mobile device-toting businesspeople a quick and easy way to file things on their devices. What it did not do was diversify to more sophisticated features that would appeal to the techie community. Barry wanted that cachet. With it he could attract the tech talent he needed to expand the Arrow platform into great things. With the loss of Zinc, he was not sure how to achieve that. Now he needed a new direction.

Never one to let grass grow under his feet, Barry decided to try out his Excelsior idea one night while having dinner with his legal counsel, Bill Morely. Barry regarded Bill, a senior partner at Arrow's law firm, as both a legal advisor and trusted confidant. Bill asked Barry questions others did not dare to ask and expect to get answers. Usually, Barry provided the answers.

On this particular night, Bill had been asking Barry about Zinc. Barry could not go there.

"Well, have you talked with them, Barry?" Bill asked after hearing Barry say once again he had no idea what happened with that deal.

"I told you. I tried and got one big 'No Reply.' They don't want to talk to us, and I am sick of asking."

"Aren't you sick of not knowing the answer?"

"No. I've quit caring. Besides, I've got better things to do with my time."

"Oh, such as what?"

"Such as moving on to the next business opportunity."

Barry went on to describe to Bill how he had been developing Excelsior, his new version of Sizzle for the legal industry.

Bill knew all too well the market Barry described. Lawyers are notoriously particular about their files. Historically, medium- and large-sized law firms had an army of finicky file clerks to tend to the mountains of paper generated by their lawyers and staff. With the army of clerks often came a field general who applied with Prussian precision a heavy-handed regime of filing rules.

Young lawyers who wanted a career at their law firms quickly learned never to mess with those rules. Over time, as paper files became digital, the armies and their generals started to disappear. What did not disappear was the propensity of lawyers to generate massive documentation. What also did not change was the resistance of lawyers to organizing their documents, digital or not.

A couple of weeks after the Zinc project ended, Arrow engaged the services of a former field general from a law firm records department to develop a law firm filing application. Its goal was to allow lawyers to send documents quickly into digital folders. The ultra-organized general did a brilliant job mapping out logical categories, subcategories, file numbers, and even keywords that recognized from a document title where the file should go. Even more brilliant, to counter the Trash debacle each document traveled with a filing history. Typing its name into the system produced a record of where each of the documents had landed.

The Excelsior opportunity excited Barry. He saw the legal filing market as deep, wide, and endless. Lawyers would never give up their acres of documentation. They also would never, with rare exceptions, want to spend any mental time on filing.

Bill assumed the neutral expression of a seasoned lawyer as he listened to Barry's description of Excelsior. Finally, he raised his hand and said, "Well, you certainly have captured the essence of the lawyers and their files. I can see why you are interested. I also can't help pointing out, however, the minor matter of lawyers having a reputation for being not only late, but last, to adopt most things technological. They also hate to pay for them once they do."

Barry gestured dismissively. "Oh, that's merely a problem to be solved."

It was now getting late, and both men needed to go home. They wound up the conversation with the usual pleasantries, shook hands, and turned to go their separate ways. As he walked away, Bill turned his head and said, "Done as you feel you are with Zinc, you might try to not close that one out yet. You never know what you can learn."

"Sure, okay," Barry said, and sped in the opposite direction.

If Bill's comment on the slow adoption rate of the legal community bothered Barry, he quickly shook it off. A beta launch for the Excelsior project was set to happen in three weeks, and serious work remained. The developers were behind schedule, but Barry figured they would burn a lot of midnight oil to make the deadline. He had asked Simon about it at the last leadership team meeting. Actually what he said was, "Well, Simon, you of course will have your guys ready on time!" Simon responded with a lazy shrug, and the meeting went on.

Barry directed his attention to opening the Excelsior spreadsheet. He clicked across numerous tabs that laid out different regions, sizes, and types of law firms, and other parameters. Checking the formulas and thinking through the assumptions gave Barry the same kind of calm flowing through his body he felt when he left the health club in the morning. For the next five minutes he fiddled with different revenue scenarios. How great it felt that after each adjustment to an assumption, one more click produced new results instantly. *If only the world behaved as well as a spreadsheet,* he thought wistfully.

Chapter 2: Midday, Navigating the Unknown—Uncovering Hooks

Moving into the unknown to pursue bigger bets sends leaders into risky places. The possibility of failure, ridicule, loss of reputation, or even loss of job can all loom large.

Janey Trips over a Familiar Hook

Barry's moment of peaceful contemplation ceased abruptly with the appearance at the door of Janey Fahey, Marketing director. She had charged straight past Marjorie in a plume of self-importance. Marjorie generally had no problem with being bypassed. She refused to play gatekeeper, particularly when she smelled a conversation that might yield something juicy for the novel. For that same reason, she rarely bothered to close Barry's door.

While only in her early thirties, Janey had the tenacity and drive of someone with several more years of experience. She also, being a Millennial, understood the power of the social media space. She came aboard during the Sizzle 2.0 debacle and had been instrumental in guiding a strategy to mitigate the reputational harm to Arrow in the social networks.

Janey was wiry, kinetic, and smart. She tended to be confident beyond what her years of experience actually supported, something that did not always lead to the best outcome. When met with resistance, she would step around or over the person, dismissing him or her with a conspicuous eye roll. Older workers complained about her arrogance. Younger workers revered her forcefulness. Barry varied in his opinion, depending on the day.

Today, his opinion of Janey erred on the side of disliking her. He did not need to hear what he suspected she was about to say. He sighed noiselessly and watched as she cut a beeline straight from his door to a spot opposite his desk chair. Barry felt certain that if he put a traffic engineer to the task of calculating the shortest line of travel between his front door and that spot, Janey would do one better.

With Janey came Michael Marcourt, a slim, self-effacing, young man who viewed keeping Janey happy as his primary job description. While Janey cut her swath toward Barry's desk, Michael slinked around the perimeter of the office, settling down onto the edge of Barry's couch. As he did so, he spied a bowl of brightly colored jellybeans on the coffee table. Jellybeans represented Barry's one permitted departure from his gluten-free, non-GMO, low-carb regime. Checking to make sure no one was watching, Michael leaned into the bowl and started to forage for the prized licorice jellybeans.

Meanwhile, Janey started in on Barry. "What's this I hear about us not responding to Porter on its questions? You know how critical that company is to our brand building. We have worked months to bring Porter to a place where they're asking us only a handful of last-minute questions and you blow it off."

"Excuse me?" snapped a surprised Barry. "And where might I ask, are you getting your information?"

"I just saw Arnie in the hall, and he said he was not getting serious support from you."

"Did you happen to ask what he meant by that?"

"I didn't need to. I know what you are doing!"

"And what exactly would that be?" Barry's attitude changed from minor annoyance to mild curiosity.

Janey leaned a few inches over the upper left quadrant of Barry's desk. "If you really wanted this deal, you'd be all over the questions yourself. Instead you're letting Arnie run around trying to find out things that on any other deal you'd be chasing down yourself. Your head seems to be someplace else!"

Barry by this time could not help noticing he was feeling less like a participant in this conversation and more like a member of an audience watching a badly acted play. He tipped his head slightly to the right and gazed at Janey. "Else? And where would that be?"

"I don't know, but wherever it is, I think you don't want us to win this deal!"

"Really? Why is that?" By now, this badly acted play amused Barry.

"Because . . ." She peeked back at Michael for support. Michael dug his head deeper into the jellybean bowl. Janey frowned and turned her face back at Barry. "Because it was I who found this deal with my hot tip on Porter's search for a vendor. You don't believe that I can bring in something that is really great! And, and . . . I also think you don't want us working on anything unless it is your deal!"

The room became quiet, except for the clacking noise of Michael working his way through the jellybeans.

"Oh, I see," Barry said finally, wondering what had happened to the age of respecting one's elders. He rarely liked to think of himself as even remotely old, although as someone in his late forties he was starting to worry. More to the point, he knew he encouraged a democratic culture where people could talk freely regardless of rank, but this was different. Why did Janey have to personalize things? The future of the Porter deal had nothing to do with her competence, much less her value as a human being. Her going there did not fill him with confidence about her executive prospects. He felt sure he did not take credit for the work of others. That seemed like a completely bogus claim.

On one count, she was right. His mind was somewhere else. Losing the Zinc deal had hit him hard. He did not doubt that he had a role to play in that negative outcome, but he did not know what he did or did not do that caused it. What was worse was he did not buy his own rationalization that the client relationship ended because Zinc had failed to deliver timely programmatic requirements. Sure, had they been faster with the requested information, the project would have gone more easily, but that didn't seem like enough to cancel an entire project.

The Arrow team had reacted to their dismissal with shock and anger. If Simon had his theories, he wasn't sharing them. Barry thought that something went south in the scoping process. He had heard about the many questions his team had asked and Zinc's resistance to answering them. For a while he thought Zinc was merely being difficult. That company had a reputation for its combative culture, mirroring its debate-king CEO. The more time went by, however, the more Barry was nagged by the feeling it was not the whole story. His development people were also suspicious.

Thinking back on the trouble that Arrow had getting information, Barry's mind kept turning over a thought that would not leave him. It was the nature of the slowness. It felt as if Zinc had never really bought into the project. Given the many months it took to negotiate that contract, Barry could not fathom why its implementation would encounter a subtle but noticeable lack of commitment from the client. Throughout that time, something had gnawed at him. Had the client found something it liked better and decided to passive aggressively weasel out of the deal? Not knowing what really went on with Zinc and now these questions about it from Porter troubled Barry, more than he wanted to admit. Were the two things related?

Ray Sniffs after the Unknown

There are those who thrive in the unknown. They often are not executives and do not aspire to the role. Nevertheless, their willingness to explore beyond what is in front of them can lead them to discoveries that influence others to travel deeper into the labyrinth. A smart organization will support their exploration into the unknown and see it as a positive rather than a negative disruptive force.

Ray Hillman leaned into a stack of desk chairs to push them toward a corner of the Arrow musty basement storage space. The recent business challenges had led to a reduction in force. In Ray's world, a RIF merely meant that he had more furniture to move into the basement until the next growth uptick. It also meant, depending on who left, that he might be losing valuable sources of company gossip.

Ray had been with the company since the beginning. He originally managed its small warehouse when Arrow sold briefcases and other organizing accessories to complement the filing systems sold by the company. That revenue stream did not last. Soon after Arrow opened in 2005, the world became digital. Conventional briefcases, calendars, and other physical organizers quickly lost their appeal.

When the organizing-accessories business dried up, Ray remained. Early on, he succeeded to become so enmeshed in the social fabric of Arrow that Barry decided to assign him to facilities management. His duties included office moves, maintenance, repairs, and, his personal favorite, installation of whiteboards. That last one allowed him to linger in an office long enough to chat up its occupant.

Ray, a handsome, athletically built guy, had a dry wit and style of listening that encouraged people to talk to him. He was so popular that a steady stream of people would flow into his basement office, plop down into one of the surplus chairs, and share a wide range of things. Ray loved the social life. Many people at Arrow had figured this out. One by one they would find a reason to visit the basement to "check on the supply chain." This setup suited Ray fine. Not only did it give him unofficial job security, he also relished learning the grittier details of office rumors.

Everyone at Arrow loved talking to him, that is, except Marjorie who had her own information sources to mine. Her tolerance of Ray depended on how much information she needed from him. As far as she was concerned, that was his only purpose at the company.

Standing next to the pile of chairs, Ray stopped to rest. While he was doing so, his eyes lit on a sticky note sticking off the side of the drawer of a workstation he had moved out of the Sales Department last week. He leaned over and pulled it off to give it a closer inspection. The barely legible scrawl said, "Call Porter about Zinc!"

Porter . . . Cathryn Porter? Ray wondered. He thought about it some more and then remembered hearing from Arnie, the ever-earnest junior sales exec, how Arrow was hotly pursuing the Porter business, and things weren't going so well.

Ray chuckled as he remembered his cynical pursuit of Cathryn Porter when they were in high school together. He was the ultra-handsome class hunk. She was the class nerd, straight from central casting with stringy, dishwater brown hair shoved behind her ears, crooked glasses, and sensible shoes.

Cathy, as she was then called, had limited social skills. She could line up subject and verb when she talked, but she could not read faces or situations to save her life. When she chose to interact with others, she had a wet, goofy sense of humor only she found funny. After telling one of her pointless jokes, she would explode into a bray of laughter, scattering her audience in a near panic.

Nevertheless, Ray was a little intrigued. He was never short of girlfriends, but Cathy reminded him a bit of his nerdy mom, whom he loved dearly. She had a sense of humor Cathy lacked, but it was the nerdy part that interested him. He decided to give Cathy a try as sort of a social experiment. If it failed, he could always backfill with a cheerleader or two.

Cathy, being socially obtuse, did not guess Ray's intentions. She was also smart and instantly suspicious when Ray asked her out. She might not have realized how little her humor was appreciated, but she recognized she was hardly a cover girl. Ray persisted in asking her to go out with him. Finally, flattery overtook her good judgment.

They went out a few times to movies, cheap meals, and other low-key activities. Ray, being a good listener even as a teenager, encouraged Cathy to talk, and talk she did, and did. While Ray actually found her interesting, he soon got past the novelty of dating a nerd. He wanted to switch back to someone with more compelling physical attributes. He reached this conclusion one night after he finally gave her a perfunctory goodnight kiss. She immediately circled her arms around him, gripping so tightly he feared his ribcage would splinter. She was excited. He was horrified. The next day he dropped her without ceremony.

His sudden departure left Cathy angry and confused. Ray had no such confusion. He quickly moved on, finding himself a cheerleader. He and Cathy never spoke again, something that suited them both. After high school, with the intervention of several business and beauty consultants, Cathy underwent a metamorphosis, doffing the nerdy clothes and demeanor to become "Cathryn," an ultra-cool, attractive, and collected modern woman.

Ray went on to be, well, Ray, enjoying an underachieving work style that left him with time and energy to pursue his number one passion—coaching his daughter's soccer team. Ray was a great athlete in school. Combining his love of sports and his daughter provided an ideal combination. He also loved his wife, who had never been a cheerleader and excelled in her studies. She was also beautiful and fun.

Back in the present, Ray stared at the sticky note. "Hmm, I wonder what's up? I better go hang a whiteboard or two in Sales." He grabbed his drill kit and moved toward the elevator.

Barry Disengages and Remains in the Known

An easy way to avoid the scariness of the unknown is to disengage from it. Jumping into something else that moves you away from the problem can give you short-term comfort, but it will not solve the mystery of what is happening that is having a negative impact on your business.

In Barry's office, Janey continued to glare at Barry, who ignored her. His head swirled with the gnawing anxiety that rose whenever he thought about the Zinc deal. He kept stealing a glance at the Excelsior spreadsheet in search of comfort. He quickly read across a couple of rows and thought about their significance. It calmed him enough to return his attention to Janey.

Taking on a stern tone, he said, "The Porter deal is a matter of highest priority for this company. Your job right now is to go work with Arnie and Nigel, if you can find him, to answer the Porter questions. You got it? And take Mr. Jellybean here with you!"

Even Janey knew when it was time to fold. Michael had already fled out the door. Janey pivoted on one foot and marched out of the office with firm, deliberate steps. Barry watched her depart, noticing the stiffly held shoulders above the firm stride.

Marjorie did not acknowledge Janey as she left. Instead, once she disappeared from view, Marjorie leaned forward in her chair and peered discretely in at Barry to see how he was doing after dealing with that obnoxious young woman. Coldblooded as she could appear, Marjorie actually cared a lot about people, particularly hardworking, smart people like Barry who were basically decent folks.

She heard him exhale loudly. He remained still for a moment. Finally, he turned his head toward his computer screen where a spreadsheet was open. He stared into the screen, mumbled, "Hmm," inserted a number, and hit the return button. Lowering his eyes to the bottom of the page, he smiled at the recalculation. He rolled his chair closer to the screen to study something, nodding as he did so. Marjorie watched as he then settled against the back of his chair and decided he would be okay.

Arnie and Simon Stall Out in Their Hooks

In a darkened corner of the third floor, Simon, the vice president of Engineering, worked his way through a mound of taco chips and salsa while staring into the third of his four monitors. Munching away on a chip, he brooded on a line of code that kept pointing the wrong direction.

One could not help comparing Simon to a pinecone—roundish, amorphously shaped with a prickly exterior. Simon eschewed social niceties, figuring his brilliance as a coder gave him an exemption card to all that manners stuff. He did not find most people interesting. Instead, he lived in the cyberworld where he whiled away endless hours, often on task. Other times he wandered onto sites related to dark matter. Ah, space, the final frontier. Why had he been born too early?

Given his general disinterest in people, Simon was liked by virtually no one, except perhaps his mother, and Charles Kramer, chair of the Arrow board of directors. Charles and Simon shared a deep passion for dark matter. They fired messages back and forth daily, feasting on the latest dark matter research.

Simon was reading a missive from Charles that had just popped up on his second monitor when Arnie tentatively tapped at the door. At first, Simon ignored him. If whoever was there wanted something enough, they could knock again, louder. This Arnie did, then cleared his throat.

"Uh, Simon, you got a minute?" Arnie realized immediately that was exactly the wrong approach.

"Of course not," Simon did not take his eyes off his computer screen. He went on noisily crunching his chip and reading Charles' message. Arnie stayed rooted to the spot, not knowing quite what to do. After another minute or so had passed, Simon could feel Arnie's continued presence. He slowly rotated his chair toward the door.

As he turned, a dribble of salsa leaked out the side of his mouth. He grunted and leaned over to the toilet paper roll mounted on a wall dispenser to the right of his four monitors. He yanked off a couple of squares and wiped his mouth. He was rather proud of his dispenser, a sleek, modern design he had bought for a fraction of its original cost from a distressed condominium developer.

He finished blotting his chin and tossed the toilet paper to the side. Tilting back in his chair, he laced his fingers across his roundish midsection and stared blandly at Arnie. Arnie still stood in the doorway, leaning against its frame for support.

"I suppose you will not leave until I give you said minute. So what do you want?"

Arnie took a couple of steps into the room. In a voice sounding more like a choir boy than a rising executive, he started to describe the Porter proposal and its critical importance to Arrow.

Simon abruptly interrupted him, "Oh, puhleazzeee! This might have escaped your notice, but I run the Engineering function here and probably know more about the Porter deal than you ever will. What do you think I do all day?"

Arnie resisted replying, "Eat and IM?" Instead he decided to cut to the chase. "Porter wants to know the cost per developer on our last three deals."

Simon's facial expression went from bland to bored. "Oh, do they now? Whatever for?"

"I don't know. I assume they are comparing our cost competitiveness to somebody else's."

"How would they even know what they are looking at? If they did, they could do this work themselves and not bother us with it."

"Oh, come on, Simon, be reasonable. It's not the first time we've been asked for this information. Would you *please* give me something?" *Honestly*, Arnie thought, *does Simon get paid a bonus for being so exasperating?*

"I'll think about it," Simon said, being exasperating. What he actually was thinking about was the last time Barry wasted his time with that stupid Excelsior project. Simon viewed that project as dead on arrival. He had worked with the legal market in a previous life and had no doubt that lawyers would not embrace any kind of digital filing system. It would require taking behavioral risks that lawyers don't take and cost money they wouldn't spend. Instead of sharing this opinion with Barry, however, Simon decided to "slo mo" the Excelsior development work, finding lots of other things to do instead.

Arnie, during this time was summoning as much junior executive energy as he could; he took a deep breath, stood up straighter. "Simon, we don't need you to THINK about it. We need you to DO something about it!"

"I'll think about that too," Simon swiveled back to his second monitor without so much as a backward glance.

Arnie could see this conversation had reached the end of its useful life and left feeling utterly exhausted.

Marjorie and Ray Compete for the Unknown

Ray came whistling back from the Sales Department after a most satisfactory visit. The whiteboard was installed and information collected. A young assistant he had befriended cornered him to tell him how stressed Arnie was. He had been heard running around the halls moaning something about having to explain the Zinc deal.

Zinc, thought Ray. *Wasn't that where that arrogant Mark Miller worked?* He'd see Mark from time to time on the soccer field. His daughter played on the same team as Ray's daughter. He usually had his head stuck into his phone. He'd break off from a call from time to time when his daughter made a goal or more likely when she missed one. He'd talk to other fathers, that is, those who were in the corporate world. Mrs. Miller was nice. She always greeted him warmly. Then they would chat about their daughters, soccer, and life in general. You can learn a lot alongside a soccer field.

Before returning downstairs, Ray made a detour by Marjorie's desk. Marjorie did not share others' enthusiasm for Ray. Aside from resenting his protected status of holding a job that did basically nothing, Marjorie felt he always seemed to have an agenda. That latter feeling was a tad hypocritical. Marjorie also loved to collect company gossip. Sitting outside the office of the CEO gave her great source material. Each bit that floated or fired through the CEO's door got happily inserted into the novel. She hoped eventually to chuck the daily grind of placating others and live off the royalties of her first of many novels. For now, the grind provided good source material, some entertaining diversion, and, she sighed, a paycheck.

In the entertaining diversion category was her ongoing contest with Ray. A fiercely competitive woman, she could not resist jousting with him over who had the better finger on the company pulse. Throughout the years, they developed a favorite blood sport they called the Daily News, where they would compare notes on what they had learned about Arrow current events, rumors, and daily dramas. Then they moved on to the main event, which was the scoring thereof.

First, they assigned to each snippet of information a temperature rating according to how surprising the news would be to different levels of company insiders—rank and file, leadership team, and the board. Next, they rated the level and reliability of the source. If the information on a previous piece of information turned out to be true, extra points were added to its final score. Finally, came the rating for their favorite category, labeled Juiciness, also known as the "titillation factor."

The fact that all these scores were totally subjective never got in their way. They would fiercely debate each component as if it actually mattered.

Marjorie kept the tally sheet of their ratings on top of the file cabinet behind her desk. Aside from breaking the boredom of the day, it gave her additional book content. For Ray, the game harkened back to his happy, high school, sports days and all the scorekeeping that went on there, on and off the field.

"A Zinc stink, eh?" said Ray, teeing up a Daily News challenge.

Marjorie smiled back, close-lipped in sphinxlike fashion. Finally, she opened her mouth and said, "Yeesss . . ." The next step was the dance of who knew what, when, and how much followed by the scoring thereof. They went methodically back and forth, point by point. At the end of three or four exchanges, they realized that neither knew much beyond Arrow losing the Zinc business and somehow Porter caring about it. They called this round a draw and assigned equal points on the tally sheet. Ray left for the basement. Marjorie turned back to her novel. Clearly both had more investigating to do.

Ray Continues to Sniff at the Door of the Unknown

Thinking further on Zinc, Ray remembered something he heard the week before at his daughter's soccer game that might be of interest to the Arrow executives, especially in the Engineering group. With that in mind, Ray decided he needed to find an excuse to see Simon.

The excuse conveniently materialized when Ray arrived back in the basement. A member of Simon's team came down to complain that the whiteboard in Simon's office where they did their brainstorming was so filthy that they had a hard time reading what they wrote. Valuable information kept disappearing into the grunge. Ray decided to take matters into his own hands and showed up in Simon's office, announcing that he was doing routine "maintenance" on all the company whiteboards. Simon continued to peck away on his keyboard.

While Ray scrubbed off several sedimentary layers of marker pen and splotches of taco sauce, he looked over his shoulder at Simon and said, "Oh, by the way, I heard the funniest thing at my daughter's soccer game over the weekend." Simon didn't move or show any other sign he was listening. Ray decided to go on. "Well, as you might know, Mark Miller's kid plays on my daughter's team. He never talks to me except about how to improve my coaching. His wife is nice. I talk with her about all kinds of things." Still no response, as Simon kept clicking on his keyboard. "Anyway, yesterday, I asked whether her daughter was going to be a techie like her dad. She responded, 'Techie? Mark a techie?' She snorted and then said, 'He flunked the one computer science course he took in college! He's a business jock who is smart enough to know that tech makes money.'"

At this point, Ray thought he detected Simon stir ever so slightly in his chair. Ray waited for a few seconds for a response. When none came, he decided his time was up. He wiped up the last taco sauce stain and left, wondering how long it would take for the whiteboard to need emergency care again.

Simon Disengages

Simon actually had been listening, closely. Mark Miller flunked computer science...Hmm...How that guy loved to strut around like he was Mr. Tech Executive! He couldn't even pass an intro-ductory computer science class! Now that was rich! Wouldn't Charles love to hear this . . . But what if he didn't? Charles was funny when it came to talking about other companies. You never knew what other boards he was on. Besides, why would Charles care if Simon knew stuff about executives from Arrow competi-tors? He only liked to talk about dark matter. So why bother? At the same time, Simon was sick of his pigeonhole where nobody appreciated his brilliant work, much less gave him the senior vice president title he had earned several times over.

Of course, he could pass this piece of information about Mark to Barry. Barry might actually be able to make use of that tidbit in this Porter thing and the Zinc question. He shuddered. He never knew which Barry was going to show up—Jock Boy Barry, Mr. Suave Politician Barry, Your Big Buddy Barry, Attack Dog Barry. The Barry he never saw was Mr. Observant Barry who actually appreciated what you did.

Simon had moved heaven, earth, and a couple of planets fixing that Trash debacle, coming in before ten a.m., staying up until two a.m., and missing more than a few meals. He fixed the bug, wrote the protocol to prevent its recurrence, and tossed the result up to the executive suite. The only way he knew it had been received was a message from Charles a few days later saying he'd heard at the board meeting that the Trash issue had been fixed. He assumed Simon was involved in that and wanted to say thanks.

Assumed, Simon thought. *How hard would it have been for Barry to give him a little credit at the board meeting, or, here's a concept, to me directly! He can live without this little piece of Mark Miller biography I got from Ray.*

He felt pleased with his decision and calmer that he did not need to deal with Barry Whoever-He-Was today.

Simon was used to not getting credit. His father chaired a prestigious department at MIT and had achieved a towering reputation in his field. He gave Simon his high-powered brain, but with it came no positive reinforcement for his son. When in eighth grade, Simon, a shy boy, marshaled the courage to tell his father about a prize he received at school for a unique approach to programming, his father said, "Well, what else are you supposed to be doing in school? That's why we pay that exorbitant tuition!" Given that response, Simon retreated into the wonderful, human-free world of astrophysics.

His mother tried from time to time to pull him back to earth, plying him with his favorite foods. He liked food and his mother. She meant well, and that was worth something. Actually, it was worth a lot. When his father's remoteness proved to be too much, he would retreat into the kitchen where his mother combined her day job of bookkeeping for a local nonprofit with baking.

Within a few minutes of his appearance in the kitchen, she would deliver up some warm, delicious, baked item and ask him how his day was going. Telling her it was "not so good" could lead to a really uncomfortable conversation. You never knew where that would end up. What if she tried to intervene with his father and ask him to be nicer to his son? Then what? Better stick to eating cookies, smiling broadly, and making idle chitchat.

Arnie Hits More Walls of Resistance to the Unknown

Arnie dragged down the hall after his unsuccessful interview with Simon. He should have expected it. Simon was, after all, Simon. That Simon behaved that way with everyone did not make Arnie feel any better. To gather the information Barry needed for the Porter deal, Arnie was stuck dealing with that institutional roadblock.

Dealing with difficult people was hard enough for Arnie. He hated unpleasantness. What he hated even more was having to debate with them or anyone for that matter. Rather than staying in the fray, his first instinct was either to pretend he agreed with the other person or, better yet, bolt in the opposite direction.

This well-honed conflict avoidance rarely served him well. In the moment, he experienced the relief that came from dodging disagreement. After the moment, he found himself left with nothing but an unsolved problem that he would either have to solve on his own or work around.

Arnie was all too familiar with combative environments. He grew up with four brothers and a sister who regarded arguing as their favorite pastime. That did not mean that any issues got resolved. They viewed giving an inch to any of the others as failure, a despicable display of vulnerability. His parents stayed to the side of all this, believing that competition among children was normal, and it was best if they learned to work things out on their own.

The children did not work things out. Arnie hated arguing and would not go there. With nothing ever resolved, what was the point? Instead, he wanted to stay as far from it as possible. He constructed of life of pleasantness. He chose sales, because that was the place in business where people tended to be on their best behavior. After all, to make a sale, people have to like you, or so he thought. When on a sales call, that perception panned out. However, he was now discovering that between sales calls, life was not quite so agreeable. Nobody warned him about the petty interdepartmental disputes, corporate politics, and dysfunctional people in general that occupied a surprisingly large percentage of business life.

Usually, Arnie adopted a strategy of socially agreeable perseverance, pleasantly asking and cajoling until he got what he needed. That approach generally worked. However, sometimes it did not, like with the non-conversation he had with Simon. Now he had the situation of not being able to deliver one of the most important responses needed for the Porter proposal.

He also was growing angry. Arnie liked to avoid not only anger in others, but also anger within himself. It was too dark, too difficult. Now as he trudged slowly down the hall of the third floor, he could feel a nasty, close feeling of being penned in by something he could not identify.

Argh! I hate this feeling. I HATE it.

"What do you want, Marco?" This last question flew out of his mouth, as Marco suddenly appeared in front of him.

Marco, the vice president of Operations, a hardworking, gracious man with a cherubic face, provided the project glue that supported Sales in its account management for the large Arrow customers. Without his well-documented systems and strong sense of responsibility, Arrow could often have been in a world of hurt with its ever-changing and demanding customers. For that reason, Arnie often dealt with Marco.

Choosing to ignore Arnie's unusual angry tone, Marco said, "I hear the Porter deal heated up."

"Uh, yeah." Arnie struggled to recover his game face. He felt embarrassed by his bad mood and certainly did not want to impose it on the gracious Marco. "We, uh, have some information we have to hunt down for them by the end of today."

"End of today? We only got the request this morning. Whoa. What's with that? Anything I can do to help?"

"Actually, we need you to ask Claudia's crew for profit-margin information on three of our recent projects."

"That doesn't sound too hard. Anything else?"

"Not off the top of my head right now, unless . . . unless you have any intel on what the urgency is all about over there at Porter." Arnie remembered that Marco used to work with one of the Porter senior managers when Marco and he were at another company.

"Let me see what I can find out. I'll get back with you shortly."

"Thanks." Arnie felt relieved to have been rescued from his moment of dark introspection.

With renewed energy, Arnie returned to the quest. He decided to go for the low-hanging fruit among the Porter questions. The IP issue had to be relatively straightforward. It also would feel good to check one item off the list. He headed toward the Arrow Legal Department on the north end of the second floor of the building. While the rest of the building favored the modern ochre color chosen by Barry, the Legal Department chose a muted gray blue that signaled a subdued atmosphere. As he approached the hushed hall where Janelle and her staff resided, he could hear the authoritative voice of Janelle.

Janelle was calling through the open door of her office to Joyce, the long-suffering Legal Department assistant.

"Joyce! Is it your impression that the new deli you have been using of late has decided to retain not-for-profit status? It's happened again! I specifically asked for a Mediterranean chicken salad with dressing on the side. Instead I get this marinated glob of vegetables drowning in vinaigrette. I also asked for no bread or chips and, guess what, I got both! Do they have a hearing problem over there? Would you please take this swamp of a salad back to its original owner and bring me what I actually ordered? And don't forget the receipt."

A harried-looking Joyce trotted into Janelle's office, snatched up the rejected lunch container, and disappeared quickly out the door.

Janelle started to sigh loudly, but caught herself mid-sigh when she saw Arnie standing at her door. "Ah, Arnie," a radiant smile traveled across her face. "What brings you to these hallowed halls?"

Arnie returned her smile and said, in a tone of forced merriment, "Sorry to hear about your salad, Janelle."

"Yes, it seems finding a decent meal these days has become another of life's great challenges. This one at least I can solve. Now, I assume you didn't come to this end of the building to give me sympathy for my salad issues. What do you need?"

Arnie explained what was going on with the Porter proposal and the question about who would own the IP. Janelle listened attentively, taking meticulous notes. That is, until Arnie told her that they needed an answer in time for the Porter board meeting that night.

Janelle put down her pen. Her face took on a ferocious expression. "Well, that's silly. We have not been involved in this Porter proposal. We could not possibly give you an answer to this question without proper information and adequate time to evaluate it. A few hours? No, no can do. If you would send us a copy of the proposal and the relevant materials, I could put someone on it later this week and give you something early next."

"But, Janelle, we don't have until next week. We have until six this evening."

"Well, I understand you have a situation, but we have several other pressing problems in the queue. They—"

"But this comes from Barry."

"As do all the others," a sharp edge crept into her voice.

"But this is not any other proposal, this is the Porter proposal! We really need this one!" Janelle's stubbornness maddened Arnie, although he did not say so.

"I am so tired of Barry thinking we are an assembly line down here. He hasn't a clue how complicated these issues are!" She realized she was coming on rather strong, so she took a deep breath. "Well, if Barry wants it moved up in priority, he knows how to ask. Right now, I need some lunch!"

Janelle motioned Arnie toward the door.

Arnie took his cue, having run out of options. Nothing more could be achieved at this meeting. And this was supposed to be the easy one. *Phew! Small wonder Barry refers to the Legal Department as the legal dragons.* He felt disappointed, because now he had to go back to Barry with empty hands. Anger pulled at him again, causing him to heave a deep sigh. *No time for this self-exploration stuff,* Arnie thought and picked up his pace.

Janelle Avoids Her Life Story

With Arnie gone, Janelle sat quietly in her office for a few minutes. She felt bad about the way she behaved with him. He was a nice person with an impossible job. Working for the useless, invisible Nigel, Arnie had the thankless work of picking up all the pieces that others tossed on the floor.

She knew what that was like. She grew up in a household with her parents and a younger sister and brother. Her mom worked as an artist who loved to paint and create collages. Their entire ramshackle Victorian house served as her studio throughout which she blithely strewed her materials and various projects, using every available surface, including the floor. Dinner, when her mom got around to it, often was served on one half of a hastily cleared kitchen table. The other end of the table held jars of paints and brushes soaking in juice glasses. Her mom was generally good-natured, chattering with her children in surges. Then she would disappear back into her projects and not re-emerge for hours, even when she was in the same room with them.

Janelle's father worked as an accountant for a local construction company. He had spent his entire career there. His coworkers adored him. He worked hard, was always helpful, and produced carefully assembled, precise reports. The common refrain about him at his company was, "if something is wrong in a report, you made the error, not Howard." Janelle's father, Howard, was embarrassed by this comment, but had to admit that it probably was right. His own father kept the books at a local tool company. A stern man, he had zero tolerance for error. He raised Howard, his only son, with a strong perfectionist fervor. Howard lived in dread of his father ever catching him making a mistake.

Howard passed this drive for perfection on to Janelle. While he was more like his mother in demeanor—she was always kind and supportive, even to her fierce, driving husband—Howard saw a high degree of precision as the ticket to love and safety. He recognized early in her life that Janelle had a highly analytical mind. She also showed a strong drive toward order. Whether she came into the world like that or ended up that way in response to her chaotic mother was impossible to tell. Whatever it was, Howard encouraged Janelle to capitalize on it. Law provided a perfect place to apply that propensity.

Janelle grew up unaware of her grandfather's legacy. She only knew that her father said little about him. The few times she had met her grandfather, she noticed how nervous and tentative her dad would become. It mystified her, as the father she knew was an even-tempered, calm man who loved his artist wife and their children deeply. The chaos created by his wife at home did not seem to bother him. He had order at work, and that was enough. Still, there was that undercurrent of exactitude that emanated from him when he talked with Janelle about matters related to school and later on to career.

Janelle's siblings did not share her love of order. They took more after their mother's way of being. While neither became an artist, both of them approached life in a more casual, unplanned way than their older sister. Her brother possessed great mechanical abilities that stretched from cars to electronic equipment. His talent for pulling things apart and reassembling them into better working order amazed people. It allowed him to pick up jobs whenever he needed them, then quit when he got bored, which was often. Janelle both admired and resented his talent for the freedom it gave him to be irresponsible.

Her sister pursued a more nurturing route. She married her high school sweetheart right out of school and quickly had three children. Currently, with all three now in school, she had returned to school for a teaching degree. Janelle approved of that.

Janelle did not approve of having to mop up after chaos all the time. She shared her feelings about it one night a couple of weeks ago when she and Claudia went out for an after-work drink. They did not often socialize together, but when they did, their bond as the only two women senior executives at Arrow and, for that matter, in the local tech industry, led them to talk more freely than in the office.

Janelle described her family to Claudia and how her father's love for her mother took priority over domestic organization.

"I too love my mother, and my father, but the chaos drove me nuts." Janelle swigged the last of her Merlot and signaled the waiter for another. "So, that left me to take on the shopping, cooking, and getting my siblings to school on time, each with a bag lunch. My mom would help when she was not otherwise buried in a project. Her version of help was to throw together a bag lunch with stale potato chips, a can of juice, and maybe some crackers and cheese. Not exactly what I'd call a menu for healthy growth. It fell to me to make sure decent nutrition went into those bags."

"Why you?"

"Because order matters to me. I'm good at it. My dad knew that when he suggested I go to law school. It fit me to a T. I did really well there and landed a job at a major law firm immediately after graduation."

"Yes, I remember. That must have been a big day for you when that firm gave you an offer."

"Definitely. I worked there ten years helping to move startup firms toward maturity. It was great. But after the Arrow financing deal, when you and Barry offered me the general counsel job, I got really excited. How could I not leap at it?"

"Actually, my head goes in the opposite direction. I know you liked our deal, but you were really successful at your firm."

"I was, but I was also bored, ready for a switch. Working in a law firm was a great way to hone my legal expertise. What really drove me crazy was how badly lawyers manage their business. I thought once I became a partner I could have an impact on firm management and cure its chaos. Instead I ran up against total resistance to order. It was like being back home. Lawyers despise any system that they do not personally control themselves. No firm governance could counteract the strong drive for autonomy found in most lawyers."

Claudia laughed. She knew enough lawyers to recognize the truth of this last observation.

Janelle continued, "Moving in-house to a startup looked like a great opportunity to influence how a business was put together. I loved that possibility. It helped me push through the fear of leaving a prestigious law firm to join a scrappy young business that had yet to prove itself."

"I hate to ask, but how's that working out for you?" Claudia was fascinated by what Janelle was saying. She could not help thinking about her own career questions. She waved to the waiter to refill her glass.

"Well, for sure it has had its moments, but I still believe I can have an impact here. What that is, I don't know. I do like being a decision maker rather than an outsider who merely catalogs legal risks for clients."

The two women moved on to comparing notes on the cost of housing, their upcoming vacations, and what Simon could do if he half applied himself to reducing their IT headaches.

Today the immediate reason for Janelle's unhappiness was missing her lunch. She also felt unhappy with Barry for the chaos he created. He had so many priorities, all equally weighted, or so it seemed. How on earth could her department possibly do a proper job with all the competing projects he tossed her way? She was always harping at Barry about his lack of clear priorities. He liked to experiment with ideas and she did not, always thinking in her lawyerly way of all the bad consequences that could result from such ideas.

At the same time, without Barry's wild ideas, where would they be? She actually liked some of them, but had no idea where to take them. Further, what would happen if they failed and, worse, her credibility if she was attached to them? It was easier to criticize and keep the company out of trouble. But now there was this Porter thing. Yes, she thought, it is important to the future of the company. Arrow needed to broaden its reach and reputation or it would cease to grow. Then what business would Janelle have to organize? Back to the law firm? No, thank you.

In the meantime, thought Janelle, *I don't know why Arnie sets me off, but I must remember to apologize to him.* She scribbled a note on her legal pad.

Marco's Life Story Draws New Lines,
Then He Colors Carefully within Them

Arnie did better with gathering project margins. Marco came through, as expected.

Marco spent most of his time making sure that Sales and Engineering played nicely with each other to service large customer accounts. If that was not hard enough, he also had the thankless job of managing Customer Service, the group of people who fielded individual customer questions and complaints. In that role, he also had the honor of dealing with the Trash debacle. His group found itself in the crosshairs of the social media outrage, since it sat on the front line facing the many angry customers who had lost valuable files. It also left him wary of social media and its power.

Nevertheless, he was the ultimate good Arrow citizen, never complaining, at least to others. He made sure he provided excellent customer service, externally and internally. This attitude allowed him easy access to people, at least most people (there was always Simon). The Trash issue complicated his life, because he despised delivering bad news. In the account-management world, bad news is routine, and important. Nevertheless, it was easier on his digestion to say nothing to the volatile Barry, the biting Claudia, or the ever-sarcastic Simon.

He also hated dealing with staff about customer complaints, because they tended to whine a lot and make things worse. He found it simpler to handle the complaints himself. His reward was many late nights and little appreciation from his colleagues, who did not realize how much time he spent on things. He also had to face an angry wife who accused him of being married to the company, rather than to her. That was so not the truth, yet he felt stuck. What he really wanted to do was to build new, edgy project management tools to support the Arrow brand and become known for that. There did not seem to be any time for that, however. So much to do.

While he knew his family loved him, at the same time he did not feel they, and his dad in particular, saw him as capable. Marco grew up in a family who owned a regional trucking business. His father took it over from his father and spent his days, nights, and weekends continuing to build it. He felt proud of his trucking company and wanted Marco to take it over one day. Marco had no interest. Seeing and hearing all day about cargo load sizes, drivers, routes, and the latest trucking regulations exhausted him.

His friends thought he was nuts to not join the family business.

 "You have a job waiting for you and you aren't taking it? What's with that?" they'd say.

"What's with that," Marco said to his closest childhood friend late one afternoon when the two of them were walking home from a baseball game, "is that I am not interested in trucking or even trucks at all. Never was. I like technology and project managing its delivery. When I'd visit my father's office as a kid, I'd go straight to his computer and study how he organized his files."

"Your dad was okay with that?" his friend inquired.

"Sure, he thought it was a good way for me to learn about the business." The two men laughed. Marco's facial expression then became serious. He leaned over and picked up a small rock lying on the sidewalk in front of him and threw it far into an over-grown field they were passing. Staring at the field, he said to his friend, "There was another thing. I wanted to be my own man. Going into the family business seemed like a cop out. Everything there is already in place. I would just be a cog in a wheel. How could I respect myself if all I did was apply grease to wheels put in place by others, literally and figuratively?" He grinned and then his face turned serious again.

"My family did not support me entering the tech world. My dad thought techies were bad people with bad values. I respect my dad and his values, but the trucking industry is not exactly drowning in virtue. Sure, there are many hardworking, honest drivers and managers in that world. There are also a lot of corner-cutting, cold-blooded people who only see the bottom line, regardless of what it takes."

Marco went on to explain to his friend how, with begrudging family support, he entered the world of technology as a project manager. He wanted deeply to prove to himself and his parents that he could succeed in the technology world and do so with the strong values he learned from his family.

What he did not tell his friend is what happened next.

To succeed in technology, he conducted himself carefully. He worked hard to do the right thing. Being the only person from his family to enter the tech industry, he did not know the rules of how office politics worked. He also did not feel altogether safe. To succeed he needed to proceed cautiously, taking great care to do all that was expected of him. Not only did he want to succeed in his career, he also did not want to give his father the satisfaction of saying, "See, I told you so."

This approach worked until one day something happened at a company where Marco worked before Arrow. There he discovered that his manager manipulated the data on a report destined for the company board of directors to make the project appear far more profitable than it actually was. Marco was outraged. It was one thing to fail to deliver good results. It was quite another to disguise the truth.

Screwing up his courage, he voiced this opinion to Anthony, a coworker on his team. Anthony, young and eager to please his employers, decided to pass what Marco said to their manager's manager. It turned out that the manager's manager and Marco's manager were close friends outside work. The report quietly disappeared, and Marco lost his job in the next layoff, despite stellar reviews.

His father felt bad for him, but at the same time he could not resist saying, "See, I told you so." This response upset Marco. He had expected more support, even for something that happened outside of trucking. It also further strengthened his resolve to prove to his father that the technology industry was okay, and it was a good choice for him.

He landed a job within a month at Arrow, which at the time was a startup. To avoid the risk of repeating his recent past, Marco approached his new job by coloring carefully between the lines. He followed all procedures to the letter, introducing new ones only with express permission from Barry. He made it his mission to keep people happy, or, at worst, not unhappy. Then he was happy. In no way did he want to lose another job and his chance to prove his father wrong.

Claudia Glances at Her Fears

Marco was the only leadership team member who did not trigger Claudia's love of making life difficult for others, especially when they needed her. He guessed she did not think making him miserable was a good use of her time. As long as he did not ask for much, she did not mind giving him the little he requested.

Providing project margins seemed simple enough. After all, her group did not generate the data. They merely did the math. She gave Marco the margin information on three deals where Arrow had a small learning curve in terms of the requirements and the staff. That resulted in respectable and modest profit margins. What she did not do was to provide a couple of their most recent projects that were much larger, more complicated, and probably a closer fit with the Porter project. There was too much to explain there. Questions would be asked.

The last time she discussed those two recent deals, Charles had challenged her. It made her nervous, a feeling she worked hard to avoid. It felt too much like he was asking her what good she was. It was an all-too-familiar feeling she had growing up in a home with a distant father and a mother who routinely said to her and her younger brother, "Whatever you do, don't embarrass your father. He works so hard to make things go well. Your success is important to him."

Marco left her office with, unknown to him, information on three safe and unimpressive projects. Claudia, of course, knew that and sat quietly, biting her lip. It was a habit from her youth that showed up when she felt nervous. The ring of her cell phone snapped her back into action.

Marco Avoids Going outside the Lines

Arnie returned to Barry's office two hours after his last visit. Remembering Janey's comment about Arnie's complaint about him not paying attention to the Porter deal, Barry was less than pleased to see Arnie. Arnie entered the room with Marco in tow. Barry sat at his desk, methodically peeling a tangerine.

"Marco has the profit margins from Claudia, so that's one off the list." Arnie thought it was best to start with a positive headline.

Barry nodded in appreciation. He pulled a section off his tangerine. "Which deals did she give you?"

Arnie named them.

"You're kidding me. Those pissant deals? They don't represent what we can do!" Barry waved the tangerine section around like a miniature conductor's baton. Arnie's mind went blank, not knowing what to say. His eyes fixated on the waving tangerine like a cat following the flight pattern of a fly.

Marco jumped in, "Those are the deals she said were the most accurate."

"'Accurate.' And what, pray tell, does she mean by that?" Barry asked. When neither of his visitors said anything, he shook his head as if to clear it. "Oh, never mind. It sounds like one of those Claudiaisms. Let me handle that one." Then he noticed Marco and Arnie exchanging glances as if each was waiting for the other to speak.

"Is there something else?" Barry asked.

Arnie finally spoke. "Actually, yes. Marco heard from a friend he has at Porter who hinted something else might be up over there."

"What kind of 'something else'? Did you call Anthony at Porter to find out?" Barry was referring to the vice president of Procurement.

"Uh, no, but Marco did."

Barry turned his head toward Marco, "Well, Marco?"

"He wasn't exactly forthcoming. He mentioned hearing something in the executive suite about Cathryn needing to accelerate things because of some kind of 'critical window,' but he didn't know what that window was."

"Did you ask him what he could find out for you?" Barry thought he was asking the obvious.

"Anthony was really nervous talking to me at all, and I didn't want to push it."

"Well, that makes ME nervous. If something is going on that involves not only the timing but the deal itself, we need to know."

"I know, sir," Marco acted more formally when stressed. "But you never know how that guy will respond. He can be really helpful one minute and fly off the handle the next. I didn't want to upset him."

"Well, that's kind of you, but, in the meantime, we are left with a situation, and one that has to be solved pronto. Where is that useless Nigel?" Barry dismissed the two men, returning his attention to the tangerine. He stuffed another section into his mouth and chewed vigorously.

Nigel Enters the Scene, Bearing Considerable Baggage

Almost simultaneously with this query, in the downstairs lobby could be heard the rumble of luggage wheels rolling across terracotta tiles. Nigel Johnson, the vice president of Sales, had entered the building. He had been on a road trip visiting customers. He was now returning to headquarters to put in his weekly appearance.

The lanky man strolled across the floor with an air of self-assurance, his left hand holding onto the loop of the leather coat tossed over his shoulder and his right hand pulling his wheelie bag. His sandy brown hair looked as if he had been just scratching his scalp, but it was nothing a quick run through with his fingers wouldn't fix. Otherwise, he appeared polished and in charge. Nigel had a magic touch. Being out there with the customers made both them and him happy.

Returning to the Arrow office was something else. There were a bunch of second guessers who cramped his style with stupid questions and requests. He understood what was needed in the field without the complication of Engineering and Operations egos trying to strut their stuff with a barrage of useless requests. Nevertheless, the company did sign his paycheck, so he needed to make nice with the place on a periodic basis.

As Nigel approached the elevator to go to his third floor office, Janey stepped in front of him.

Janey had been watching for Nigel. She had checked with the Sales Department admin to find out when he was due to arrive. As soon as she saw him, she pounced on her quarry. "There you are!"

He turned his head perfunctorily in her direction. "Yes, and—"

"Nice timing! The Porter deal is blowing up, and you are out on one of your frolic-and-detour missions with customers."

"Oh, I see," Nigel deepened his British public school accent, a habit of his that occurred when he wanted to distance himself from a situation. "Is that how you think I spend my time? Well, that frolic and detour, my dear young lady, pays for your groceries."

Janey pulled in her breath at his condescending remark. She quickly recovered. "My groceries, as you put it, are the product of building our brand and making customers want to talk with you!"

"Oh, I get it," Nigel remained unimpressed. "And while we are here discussing your groceries, do you have a specific reason for talking to me, or are we just having a nice social chat?"

Janey gritted her teeth. "I said, the Porter deal is blowing up! We've got their board waiting for us to answer some tough questions tonight, including what happened with Zinc, and Barry is too concerned with his Excelsior deal to bother with it!"

That caught Nigel's attention. A substantial portion of his compensation came from sales commissions. The Porter deal represented a particularly fat one. He already had plans for that money, as did his wife.

"Do you mean Barry's still buried in that law-firm pipe dream when we have a live deal with Porter?"

Janey raised her hands in frustration, "As I said, he isn't paying attention!"

"Well, I guess I better pay a little visit to the fourth floor to redirect him . . . Now." Nigel caught hold of the elevator door that was closing. He jumped in and punched "3."

Claudia Remains Stuck

Up on the fourth floor at the opposite end of the hall from Barry's office, Claudia slumped in her desk chair talking in a low tone on the telephone.

"Oh. Well, yes, I understand, Daddy. You and Mom have an event at the club on Thursday night. I had hoped you could pass on a club dinner this one time. I am receiving an award at the local CFO professional association for best CFO of the year. No big deal, I know, but it would be great if you'd come . . . Oh. I see.

The Harrisons are coming with you to the club dinner? I didn't realize they were back in town. Oh, well, no big. I just thought I'd check. Yeah. Sure. I understand. Thanks. Bye." She replaced the receiver slowly.

She didn't understand and wondered if it would ever change. She had spent a lifetime trying to capture her parents' attention with her countless good deeds. No matter what she did, however, nothing seemed to work. They had their own life to lead, and lead it they did, with vigor. They didn't mind telling their friends about what a high achiever she was and smart too. This she would hear periodically from either the friends or their children, but she never heard those accolades directly.

Ironically, though, they showed interest in her children who brought out in her parents the warmth and fuzziness she never saw growing up. It's not that she didn't appreciate the attention they gave to them. She did. Granted, it sometimes drove her crazy when her children referred to Grandpa and Grandma as "the best." It deepened her resentment of her parents, given how they treated her.

At least Charles, chair of the Arrow board of directors, appreciated her. They seemed to always get along. He loved the thoroughness and precision of her financial reports. He also appreciated her strong professionalism about what was the "right" thing to do. She wished the others on her team felt that way. Most of the time, they resented it. However, if she let down on her standards, would they still respect her? And how would Charles react?

The Unknown at Work outside of Arrow

One way of dealing with the unknown is to blow past it, ignoring what is actually going on in the room. In this, executives can often confuse taking charge with not taking in reality. It works, briefly.

Porter, Inc.

Over at Porter, its namesake CEO, Cathryn Porter, was busy. She steamed down the hall to her next meeting, speaking at warp speed with her trusted right hand, Miriam. "So, what have we heard back from Arrow? We are mere hours away from the board meeting, and we've got to be ready!"

Miriam replied, "I talked with Arnie an hour ago. He said he was all over it and would be back to us later this afternoon."

"How much later? We haven't got a whole lot of 'later'."

"I know, but we did ask some really meaty questions."

"Nonsense! They should have anticipated all of them. All they have to do is to pull the reports! Call that Arnie guy and see where he is on things." Cathryn adjusted her cashmere sweater, turned, and disappeared down the hall, her 3-inch high heels clicking on the concrete floor.

She arrived at her next meeting, which was with her top developers. The meeting had been underway for some time. Cups, wrappers, and empty containers littered the table. The smell of onions, turmeric, and curry filled the air. Cathryn loved Indian food and wished she had come sooner. *Just as well,* she sighed. Her waistband was feeling a bit snug.

She entered the room and immediately took charge. "So, where are we?"

Senil Kapoor, her lead developer, sat at the end of the table. Normally, he dressed in a crisp, button-down shirt; pressed, khaki pants; and carefully combed hair. Today, his shirtsleeves were rolled up, the collar was askew, and his pants showed telltale fingerprints of greasy curry transfer. His hair looked as though it had yet to meet a comb that day.

As soon as Cathryn had seated herself, he began. "It looks promising. The beta tests with the internal focus groups came back highly favorable. The interface needs some more work. Not as elegant as we would like it, but the connection to the Cloud was quick and seamless. We are pleased with it," Senil beamed with pride.

Cathryn beamed back. Then she shifted to a more ominous tone. "Good! What's next, and how soon can you deliver it? We have a small window of opportunity here, and we've got to seize it."

Senil ignored her last remark and went on to explain the next steps, including a set of target dates. Cathryn sat quietly, except for the hands she nervously kneaded in her lap out of sight of the others. When Senil finished, Cathryn responded by changing the dates to far more aggressive ones.

Senil steadied himself with a deep breath. He and Cathryn had done the target-date dance more times than either of them wanted to count. Once Cathryn fixed her mind on something, no amount of rational persuasion would dissuade her. For sake of form, Senil mentioned a few challenges that could make her dates hard to make. To each, she responded, "make it work." He finally gave up and slowly nodded his head. His team members sat still throughout this dance, their eyes moving back and forth between Cathryn and Senil, then among one another. The room took on the air of dejection, but no one uttered a word.

Cathryn took advantage of the silence, saying "thank you" as she stood up. The meeting ended.

Zinc, Inc.

Life also looked stressed at Zinc. Two months earlier, Mark Miller, its CEO, had to explain to his board of directors that he had fired Arrow, saying only that Arrow could not fulfill Zinc's requirements. He hoped his board members would simply trust him and move on. Instead, they asked questions, a large number of them. They started with, "Well, what requirements?" and bore down from there.

Mark was used to tough questions. He usually could navigate them expertly. In a forceful style for which he was well-known, he would confidently state a concise set of strategic objectives with factual support. He had been a star debater in both college and business school. It had served him well, until now.

The Arrow matter, however, made him nervous. There was no doubt in his mind that Arrow had not done a good job of understanding what Zinc requested. The initial work led to many questions from Arrow about the Zinc platform. Zinc focused its efforts on mobile device users who liked its imaginative, albeit sometimes obscure, features. It tended to limit them to the market of sophisticated users. At the same time, Zinc prided itself on being viewed as esoteric, a cut above its competitors. It also allowed Zinc to charge a premium for its products.

Zinc hired Arrow to expand the Zinc suite with some organizing tools for files and other data. Arrow, with its long history of developing successful organizing tools seemed like a natural to create a specific file organizer for Zinc that would work with its more esoteric features. The deal was large and promised to open new markets for both companies.

Then came the questions from the Arrow engineers. Too many questions—"Why did you include this, and why did you not include that, and might we redo that navigation?" The longer they worked, the faster the questions multiplied. The Zinc developers were at first cooperative, then defensive, and finally swung into full revolt.

Mark became worried that if the project continued, his whole tech team would quit. That would be a disaster, not to mention expensive. Arrow had to go. After Mark thought about it for several days, out Arrow went, with a terse letter from him meeting the minimum cancellation notice requirements under their contract. He specified no reason.

Without the Arrow deal, Zinc had to redirect its energy and resources. Mark had his people working on it, but what happened with Arrow stayed with him like a case of the flu he could not kick.

Porter, Inc.

Back at Porter, Miriam frantically texted Arnie, "Where are things? It's been an hour and we haven't seen anything!!" she typed madly.

"Sorry. Not ignoring you. Am rushing to gather the information," Arnie typed back.

"But WHEN will we see it? Feeling major heat over here."

"Yeah, no doubt. You should see things over here. Nice deadline you guys served up."

"I know, but it is what it is. What are you going to do about it?"

"Still working on it. Be back to you in an hour with an update."

Miriam sighed heavily.

Cathryn returned. "Well?"

"They're still working on it," Miriam tried not to sound as miserable as she felt.

"Working and producing results are two different things. When are they sending us answers?"

"Arnie said he'd get back with us in an hour with an update."

Cathryn shook her head and sped off, her heels clicking like castanets.

Chapter 3: Midafternoon, Navigating the Unknown—Discovering Drivers

Nigel Searches for Driver Fuel

Having momentarily escaped the wrath of the "marketing muppet" as he called Janey behind her back, Nigel jumped out of the elevator into the safe haven of the third floor. The third floor was his floor. One end was full of noisy salespeople who buzzed around the halls, phones clasped to their ears, high-fiving one another when they heard good news, or even when they didn't. The other end of the hall was occupied by engineers who rarely talked to anyone, particularly someone like him whom he assumed they saw as a vapid salesperson. Sometimes he was inclined to agree.

As he moved down the hall, he found it hard to assume his usual vigorous stride. The closer he got to his office, the slower he walked. Nigel's work colleagues assumed he spent all his time on the road making calls. Part of that was true. However, they didn't know there were other concerns that occupied his time and attention. Turning over and over in his head were images of his last visit home.

At the breakfast table of his parents' posh country house, his father opened the most recent contractor's bill for the renovation work on his home library. He glared across the table at his wife, his face seething with anger.

"You spent $4,500 for two, 3-foot-wide cabinets? Incredible. Are we using ebony, or are we building the college fund for our beloved contractor's children? You were supposed to be supervising him. How is this possible?"

Nigel's mother sat opposite him. She had just added a teaspoon of sugar to her tea and was slowly stirring it. Finally, she replied. "Yes, George, yes I did. I mean, of course, I did my best to pay close attention to his work. But you had all these different shelf sizes and interior organizers for your various folders and—"

"Oh, I see, so it's my fault. We are over budget because I asked for too much."

"No, George, I did not say that. I merely said, the cabinets were complicated—"

Nigel's father was about to reply when Nigel stepped into the middle of the exchange.

"Enough, Father. You know how you love your detailing and how hard it is to build it. Mother is not trained in this work and still you require her to manage it. You are trained to do this stuff; so why don't you oversee it?"

"You know full well why." His father's face turned a dark shade of plum.

"What I know full well is that you spend most of your time being dissatisfied and taking it out on Mother."

Nigel's mother shook her head. "Nigel, please."

Nigel stopped. He knew the direction he was headed would

do nothing good for her. He shifted to a different strategy. He begrudgingly apologized to his father and agreed to work things out with the contractor. His father left the room. Nigel stayed with his mother while she finished her tea.

While Nigel had traveled up in the elevator to the third floor, his mind had traveled back further to being in the seventh grade. That was when his father became disabled. Once a force of nature, he ran a highly successful property development firm in England before moving to a larger company in the United States. One day while touring a construction site, a piece of temporary flooring on an upper floor broke without warning. His father fell to the unfinished floor below. He suffered an injury to his spine that put him permanently into a wheelchair. He sued the construction company for gross negligence and won a large award. However, no amount of money would restore him to his former life.

Still mentally acute but no longer having a body to match embittered his father. Rather than finding a different way to apply his keen intellect, he withdrew into his stately home and lived off the lawsuit proceeds. He spent his days overseeing the affairs of his home, reading history books, and barking at the domestic staff. He also shouted constantly at Nigel's mom and his younger sister, making them both miserable. Nigel's mom now suffered from health problems, most likely precipitated by the stress of living with her angry husband.

For Nigel, the facile social behavior that worked so well for him in a sales context did not help him deal with the dysfunction at home. All the people at Arrow knew was that he spent a lot of time on the road, and after some trips he returned far more tired than from others. Those were his trips home.

Most of the time on those visits, he worked with his mother on the household accounts (her husband did not want to touch them, considering bookkeeping too lowly), talked with his sister, and did odd errands. He also would take his father out on field trips to get him out of the house and try to improve his mood.

Whether these outings mattered to his father was hard to tell. His father did not indulge in compliments. What Nigel knew was how heavy the wheelchair felt as he pushed his father through various parks and historical monuments in the area. He did not feel he was accomplishing anything other than being a dutiful son, something his mother wanted. He knew it did little for him.

It did feed his sense of loyalty and responsibility, values that ran deep, particularly after the many years of lending emotional and physical support to his mother and sister. They needed and appreciated him. That meant a great deal and provided a beacon through dark times. He gave the same deep loyalty and support to his wife who tolerated his endless travel. She also supported him unconditionally in his need to visit his parents' home to help his mother and sister. "The least I can do is make a comfortable living for them," he said to himself.

After this latest home visit, Nigel felt, as he walked toward his office, the same heaviness he experienced pushing his father's wheelchair. What were they accomplishing here? Zinc fired Arrow for who knows why. Lots of questions got asked internally at Arrow among the Zinc development team. Nobody reached out to Zinc directly, or if they did, they were quickly fobbed off. Finally, people gave up asking. Now here they were supposedly in a new chapter and what shows up? That damn Zinc deal! Were they ever going to escape it? Talk about a futile exercise.

That was an impossible deal from the beginning. Clueless, belligerent, he thought he would never get that deal closed.

Nigel reached his office and entered his cluttered space. *This serves no purpose. I hate feeling stuck! Okay, okay. Time to do something. I don't win commissions for being stuck. I owe this to my wife for all the support she gives me. She also has the Porter commission firmly incorporated into her summer holiday plans. If Zinc is where we are stuck, let's get unstuck!*

He dumped his wheelie and steamed over to Arnie's desk for a Porter status report.

Arnie Surfaces a Situational Driver

Arnie was in a rotten mood. Having run into so many brick walls in his search for Porter answers, the anger he had earlier fought so hard to contain bubbled up and over. If he had been one of his siblings, he would have known exactly what to do with his anger. He would have blown up at whoever wandered by, and, once he vented his spleen, strolled off into the sunset leaving the bodies behind. Well, that was not going to work, because it never did. At the same time, accepting and trying to maneuver around all this stupid pushback from his colleagues also was not working.

Well, what will work? If I go on a rage fest with my teammates, they will happily respond in kind. They all seem quite good at taking defensive shots. No, that does not appeal. Being nice sure is not winning me friends or doing me any favors. I never know what shots they will take, and I feel buffeted by whatever comes at me. He shivered at the mere prospect of one of these encounters. *All I'm trying to do here is to land this deal! Somebody ought to appreciate that!*

Appreciation ... What would that feel like? He found his mind drifting toward memories of his crusty, old, Irish grandmother. She had lived with them while he was growing up. She did not seem to mind the combat zone created by his siblings. Although she did not participate, she watched. She also watched how Arnie did not enter into the fray.

His siblings never spent much time with her, or she with them. Her relationship with them was congenial, even when they were in the heat of battle. The only child to whom she paid much attention was Arnie. Arnie guessed she felt sorry for him, because he was the youngest and always at the bottom of the pile. She read him stories and asked him about his day after he returned from school. He loved his time with her. It was his personal oasis.

Something about this day at Arrow reminded him of the time he came home after being bullied by a kid at school. He could no longer remember what the kid had said. What he recalled were the painful feelings. He felt humiliated and terrible, not knowing what to say to this boy to defend himself. When he told his grandmother about it, she replied, "You have to know what you want, then you can deal with what you don't know."

That comment stuck with him, even though he was not sure what to do with it. What did he believe in? He was still thinking about it when Nigel strolled in. "Hello, mate!" he said in his most clipped accent.

Arnie remained deep in thought.

Nigel ignored Arnie's distracted expression. "I hear our friends over at Porter have thrown down the gauntlet."

Arnie shrugged. He mechanically walked through the requests and all the dead ends he had encountered.

Arnie concluded his summary by adding, "I thought we were supposed to be a team here. I have more cooperation from the Porter people, and that isn't saying much!"

Arnie was thinking about Miriam over at Porter who was incredibly hard-working and responsible. She wanted to do the right thing. She also was always pleasant.

"Nonsense. A team is what you make it." Nigel used his best cheerleading voice, with a touch of condescension. "Clearly you have some serious teambuilding in your immediate future. Get on it, man. We don't have much time."

Normally, Arnie reacted to Nigel's taunts with fear, resolving to do better. Today, remembering that bully at school, he felt that familiar pang of fear. He also experienced something different. He sure didn't need any bullying and would refuse to take the bait this time.

Instead, he took a long inward breath and frowned at his boss. Then he noticed something he had not seen before. Nigel's right eye twitched. In all the years Arnie had worked with him, he had never noticed Nigel having anything that resembled nervousness. Yet, there was this twitch, and an obvious one at that.

What was going on with him?

He put that question to the side, and instead of his usual syco-phantic, "On it!" or words to that effect, Arnie snarled through gritted teeth, "So nice to have your sympathy, maestro."

Nigel gave him a quick double take, but said nothing. Instead, he turned and proceeded to the elevator, wondering what the deal was with his junior sales rep. He had no clue. Not know-ing what else to do, he decided to forget about it. He was good about compartmentalizing some things, and he promptly did.

Arnie felt suddenly stronger. The gift from his battling family was a strong dislike of fighting for fighting's sake. What a useless way to pass the time. His grandmother was right. The impact of his family history was to form in him a strong value for bring-ing people together. He wanted to build genuine relationships rather than the superficial "going along to get along" philosophy so prevalent in the sales world.

While he was thinking about his family and his interaction with Nigel, a gray-sleeved forearm appeared above him, draped over the top of the partition surrounding his cube. There stood Marjorie. Marjorie liked Arnie. She took an almost maternal interest in his welfare, or at least as maternal as Marjorie per-mitted herself to be. He was such a decent young man.

"Hi," said Marjorie.

"Uh, hi." He was not sure what else to say. "What brings you down to the slums of the third floor?"

"Oh, I had to pick up something for Barry on the Excelsior project and thought while I was in the neighborhood, I'd swing by. Quite the day you're having."

"What do you mean?"

"Oh, I get whiffs of things from my crow's nest upstairs. I know what Porter asked us to do today and the people you have to ask for help. I can fairly well imagine the rest. How goes the campaign?"

"Lousy. Everybody has their heads in the sand. They care more about throwing up barricades than breaking them down to solve the Porter problem."

"What problem?"

"The Zinc problem! It's key to this whole thing, and the leadership team is treating it like another petty annoyance."

"I'm with you there. A lot of retreating into familiar old defenses and nothing new is getting learned."

"Amen to that."

"So, what are you going to do?"

"I dunno. I've been falling into a defensive rut myself, dodging all the pushback I keep getting to my requests . . . except . . ." He looked around to see if anyone else was listening. When he saw no one, he continued. "I got to thinking about how my old habit of avoiding conflict is only that, an old habit." He told Marjorie about the bully at school and what his grandmother said about knowing what he wanted to allow him to confront what he did not know.

"It sounds like your grandmother was a wise old lady," Marjorie said. "What do you want?"

"Well, to be super honest, my dream is to create something bigger. I really, really want the Porter deal. Not only would it expand the market for Arrow, it also would give me bigger career opportunities. If Arrow wins this deal, and I was a key part of that, it would give me the credibility I need to go after other major deals. *And*," here he looked around again to make sure the coast was clear, "I wouldn't be dependent on that bullying Nigel. I have had more than enough of that in my life, thank you very much!"

He stopped, embarrassed by his candor. He trusted Marjorie, but he was not used to admitting to himself, much less to anyone else, what he truly wanted.

Marjorie smiled slowly and warmly. "Then I think you have your answer. Go for it, and quit tiptoeing around all those people!" Arnie stood up, went around to the other side of his cube and gave Marjorie a big hug.

Nigel and Barry Revert to Dancing around the Unknown

Nigel arrived at the fourth floor corner CEO suite after a quick fueling stop at the coffee stand. Marjorie had returned from the third floor and settled back at her helm. Nigel walked straight past her with the announcement, "Coming through!" Marjorie looked unimpressed and said nothing.

Nigel in her life was at best a "neutral" source of book material. *Too obvious,* she thought. Her opinion of him had not been improved by the conversation she had a few minutes earlier with Arnie. She stared over her readers at Nigel as he passed her desk. There seemed to be something not so obvious going on today, but she could not put her finger on it. She watched as Nigel entered Barry's office and moved toward the couch.

Barry was on the phone when Nigel entered. Nigel plopped down on the couch, sinking deep into the upholstery with his hands clasped behind his head.

Barry finished his call, closed the door, and greeted Nigel. "Hello, stranger. And who might you be?"

Nigel smiled lazily. "Oh, a guy wandering by who needed a place to plant his feet," he said, parking his feet on Barry's coffee table for emphasis. He knew to miss the jellybean bowl.

"Happy to accommodate you. Is there anything else I can do?"

Never one to miss an opening, Nigel plunged in. "I hear we have a homework assignment from Porter coming due."

"That would be true. And?"

"And I hear that we are not jumping on said homework with all dispatch." Then seeing Barry's sharp expression, he realized he was slipping into dangerous territory. "At least that is what I am understanding, but, then again, I am a stranger in these parts and might not have accurate information."

Barry, annoyed by Nigel's dissembling, chose to ignore it. "Indeed, you do not. Nice of you to check in. Now I need you to stick around to plunk this homework assignment, as you call it, on to the teacher's desk before this evening."

"Naturally." Nigel made an effort to sound good-natured, although he was feeling anything but. He hated the last-minute picky details demanded by customers in proposals. He regarded them as busy work that did not improve the deal. It was stuff that could be worked out when the project was underway. Maintaining his game face, he carefully asked Barry the next question.

"I'm good with the first four questions. Routine. What's the Zinc one about? Seems rather rude."

"It certainly does. I didn't see Zinc as a relevant competitor to Porter. Zinc likes its sophisticated techie types. Porter goes for the masses."

"So I heard, but I think Cathryn is particularly interested in this one. Maybe it's the usual thing about the quality of client relationship. Are we good people to play with?"

"I thought so." Barry gazed at the ceiling to assemble his thoughts. "We have a great track record with clients. Besides, it's a well-known fact that the Zinc folks are impossible to work with. They thrive on chewing up vendors. Hard to succeed with that culture. How about drafting some kind of explanatory note for our package on all the good things we did for Zinc and how we have been wildly successful with so many others doing the same thing? We need to send this stuff over there by six this evening. In the meantime, I understand my presence is needed in

Legal to rework their priorities. Yeesh! Did Janelle never learn the fine art of compromise? She's so rigid."

Nigel smirked in agreement. He removed his feet from the coffee table and departed.

Cathryn Decides to Take Charge, or So She Thinks . . .

At Porter, Cathryn's head swam with mounting tension. The resistance of the development team to her deadlines always bothered her. She especially did not need it today when she was preparing for a major board meeting. So much rode on the Arrow proposal. She needed that information from the Arrow team and there seemed to be no pushing them faster. For the moment, she had done all she could do. She had to wait an hour for the next Arrow status update.

Best I go to the club and flush some of this cortisol out of my veins. That will help destress me.

She grabbed her gym bag and trotted over to the neighborhood health club, the same one Barry frequented in the morning. The club was a popular spot in the neighborhood. She usually saw several people there she knew from the local business community. Being in the middle of the afternoon, few were around today.

She sized up the room and saw Arrow's general counsel working up a major sweat on a recumbent exercise bike. Janelle and Cathryn shared a habit of slipping out to the health club at odd hours during the business day to work off the stress and fire up the endorphins. Occasionally they chatted, although not much beyond exchanging social pleasantries and wellness tips.

Most of the time Cathryn talked with Sarah Choi, her trainer, who had a knack of appearing on the scene as soon as Cathryn arrived.

"Hey, Cathryn! It's been a few days. That's a long time for you. What's up?"

"Oh, we are super busy. Lots and lots going on. You know how it is."

"I do, because all that need for stress management keeps you coming here. How are things going with that Mark guy?"

"Oh, he's the usual pain in the you know what. Keeps me motivated!" Cathryn jumped onto an elliptical trainer. Sarah smiled, said goodbye, and returned to her office.

Cathryn and Janelle did not speak on this day. If Janelle heard the conversation between Cathryn and her trainer, she gave no indication. In the spirit of professional courtesy, she merely nodded at Cathryn, who nodded back as they soldiered on with their respective workout routines.

Cathryn pedaled feverishly for thirty minutes, and then threw in a couple of core exercises for good measure. Seeing Janelle sparked an idea. She hustled through her routine, showered, and jumped back into her office clothes.

Feeling energized and powerful, she decided it was time to eliminate all those useless, underperforming intermediaries and go straight to the source. Barry's office was conveniently located only three blocks from the club in the opposite direction from Porter. She did not know Barry well, but well enough, working in the same industry. And, under the current circumstances, how could Barry refuse her visit?

"Time for a house call!" She marched in the direction of the Arrow offices.

She entered the Arrow building and looked with interest around the bright lobby with its wide expanse of terracotta tile. She stepped around the crack in one of the tiles and approached the receptionist. Without hesitation, Alecia greeted her by name.

"Hello, Ms. Porter." Alecia made it her business to know the players in the trendy neighborhood. You never knew when it might come in handy. "And how might we help you today?"

Impressive, Cathryn thought to herself. *I'll have to see how our receptionist measures up.*

"I would like to see Mr. Sanford. I must confess, I don't have an appointment, but if you wouldn't mind asking whether he has five minutes?"

Alecia in one smooth movement turned to her keyboard and tapped out a message to Marjorie.

Upstairs, Marjorie was putting the finishing touches on chapter nine, feeling pleased with her effort. Out of the corner of her eye she saw the popup message from Alecia with Ms. Porter's impromptu request.

Hmm . . . fresh material, and who knows what else? This would be worth tracking down Barry. She lifted herself out of her desk chair and walked down the hall in the direction of the Finance Department. Barry had gone in that direction a little earlier to talk Claudia into providing different reports for Porter.

Barry and Claudia Sink into Familiar Patterns

In moving bravely into the labyrinth toward uncertain outcomes, we can come up against our own undigested pasts. Without clarity on the places from where we have come, we may find ourselves losing our way, even when a larger goal beckons.

Barry paced back and forth in Claudia's office.

"I don't doubt, Claudia, you know your project finance. Why would I ever suggest otherwise? My question is why did you give Marco three itsy-bitsy projects that don't represent the size and reach of the work we do?"

"Now, Barry," Claudia replied in as patronizing a tone as she could muster, which was considerable. "Our bigger projects have so many irregularities in the way they were reported to us. Those engineers have never learned to tell time, much less record it accurately. They are particularly bad on the big projects where they think they have room for more sloppiness. I couldn't possibly vouch for the larger project results we have, and we have a duty to our shareholders and the board to make sure we represent ourselves properly." She sat back in her chair waiting for her pithy remarks to sink in.

Rather than letting them sink in, Barry wanted to retort by asking her why with all her headcount she had not managed to produce accurate reporting. What did she do with all her time if it was not making sure she had good numbers? Instead, he decided to sidestep the issue. It would only lead to some counterproductive remark, such as why he worried so much about the accuracy of the numbers when he couldn't keep a project long enough to produce numbers, a thinly veiled reference to the Zinc termination. He'd had that conversation before.

"Come on, Claudia. Help me out here. Certainly you have got to have something sufficiently scrubbed to deliver data to the Porter folks that supports this proposal."

"Scrubbed? That would mean 'altered'?"

"I did not say that! Quit putting words in my mouth. I MEAN you have reviewed something to a level that gives you reasonable satisfaction the data are right!"

"In other words, scrubbed."

At that moment, Marjorie appeared at the door. Unlike the rest of Arrow, she remained indifferent to Claudia's bullying. In fact, she viewed such behavior as pathetic.

Marjorie could see this so-called conversation between Barry and Claudia was well on the way to nowhere.

"Sorry to interrupt this fascinating confab." She wasn't, but knew her social conventions. "Barry, you have an unexpected visitor who has shown up, whom I think you will want to see."

Barry knew better than to question Marjorie's judgment. As soon as he heard her, he said, "Right! I'm coming." As he and Marjorie walked briskly away from Claudia's office, he said under his breath, "Thanks, Marjorie."

"My pleasure," she said, and it was. She never could resist an opportunity to cut short Claudia's controlling behavior. She accompanied Barry as far as the elevator, leaving him to return to his office alone while she descended to first floor reception.

Claudia stood in the doorway outside her office recovering from her meeting with Barry and wondering what to do next. She bit her lip while she watched Barry walk down the hall beyond the elevator. She could not help noticing how the circle of light from each of the round, narrowly spaced ceiling lights hit his head like a moving dotted line as he advanced toward his corner. When she could no longer see him, she went back to her office and sat in front of her computer screen.

For some reason, she had trouble focusing on it, her mind drifting elsewhere.

Claudia Opens a Driver Door for Janelle

Giving Barry a hard time was an easy place for Claudia to go. That way she did not have to slide down the slippery slope of debating business facts and figures with him. He was a smart man and whenever they got into a debate, he'd throw out some new twist in the road that required her to think in unfamiliar directions. She hated that. Who knows where they, and, more important, she, would end up in that conversation?

She had to admit, hard as it was, that without his pushing new ideas, Arrow would not have had as much success as it had enjoyed. She also had to confess she hated being left out all the time. Whenever she tried to enter into a discussion on company strategy, something she found enormously interesting, Barry would find a way to move her out of the room.

It's, it's . . . she could not complete the sentence. She turned her attention back to the computer screen. Somehow she could not bring its numbers into focus.

What keeps me from helping the guy? Who ends up getting hurt here?

The word "hurt" hit a nerve. It was not a word she liked to say, much less experience. She had enough of it growing up with her distant, self-absorbed parents who never could quite find the time for her. *Funny,* she thought, *I remember Barry once making a side comment that his dad was more into his golf game than his sons. What keeps him in the game?* As annoying as he could be with his dismissal of her obsession with details, he did have the right priorities. So what were hers? Her mind turned over and over, having no idea where to go next.

Strange as it seemed, she wanted to remain in that state for a while. It felt good to take a break from the crush of deliverables and reflect on something other than work product.

Something is missing from this life of mine.

A light knock on the frame of her open door interrupted her reverie. There stood Janelle, looking like her usual purposeful self.

"You got a minute?" inquired Janelle.

"Uh, yes, of course." Claudia was grateful for the break from her confusion.

"I assume you've heard about this Porter fire drill."

"Rather hard not to, although I have to say it's a bit more than a drill."

"Oh? Yeah, well, whatever," Janelle sounded momentarily disoriented. "I mean, I know this Porter deal could open a critical door for us, but—"

"But what?" Claudia leaned forward, propping her chin on her hands.

"I don't know. I feel we've been down this road before and gotten nowhere. Look what happened with Zinc!"

"Yes, and what did happen with Zinc?"

Janelle sat down across from Claudia. "Good question. Now this Porter thing comes up. First, that useless Arnie comes in this morning telling me I have to drop all my other projects to work on some IP analysis for the deal. I told him where to stuff it, or words to that effect. I guess he scampered off to complain to Barry that I wasn't playing nicely. Then an hour ago, Barry came roaring into my office asking me to push everything else to the side to make way for the Porter deal."

She clenched her fists and let them drop heavily on the desk. She stared down at her hands and said nothing. Uncurling her fingers, she raised her head and resumed in a tight voice. "I hate it when Barry comes in like a whirling dervish, with no respect for what else I have going on and expects me to fulfill his immediate request. I have fourteen projects front row center on my desk, all of which are supposedly burning hot. Now I have to assign different priorities to them to take care of Barry's need du jour. How can I possibly deliver something of high quality under these circumstances? I can't function in this chaos!" She stopped, amazed by the force of her feelings.

Claudia was taken aback by Janelle's uncharacteristic show of emotion. Usually, she spoke in a careful, intellectual manner. Claudia thought about the stories Janelle told her during their recent after-work drinks. She remembered what Janelle said about her eccentric family life where her artist mom did what she pleased, Dad indulged Mom, and Janelle ended up picking up the pieces. She also recalled Janelle saying how much she loved her family even with all its craziness. It still drained her emotionally. Claudia gained compassion for Janelle that night, and it helped her to understand better why Janelle could be so rigid at work.

With the memory of that evening fresh in mind, Claudia decided to take what was for her a big behavioral risk. "You can't?"

Janelle regarded her severely and answered evenly as if in a deposition. "What do you mean?"

As it was impossible to retract the comment, Claudia saw she had no choice but to continue. "Well, I don't mean to cross a boundary here, but I can't help thinking of something you told me about your family when you and I were out for a drink a couple of weeks ago. It seems like there was a lot of chaos there, and yet you managed to pick up the pieces fairly well. I also had the impression that it was important to you, because you care so much about your family. I know Barry's instant demands can be crazy-making when you are trying to do a good job, but that behavior is hardly unique in the work world. I wonder if you hate it because it can hit some really deep nerve endings in you, beyond Barry."

Janelle sat silently, looked briefly at Claudia, then shifted her eyes to the window. She watched the trees blowing in the March afternoon wind and marveled how the young buds clung to their branches as if they knew what they were there to do. She remained that way for what seemed like a long time. Finally, she turned back to Claudia, her eyes tearing, and said, "Touché."

The two women looked at each other and started to laugh. "Wow, aren't we complicated?" Janelle said.

"Indeed," Claudia said, drying her eyes and still laughing.

"Thanks, Claud, for the head-clearing moment. Now I think I have some IP work to do."

"Anytime."

After Janelle left, Claudia returned to her earlier ruminations. "Speaking of head clearing. I have a little of my own to do."

Cathryn and Barry Meet Each Other, and More

With unusual ceremony, Marjorie escorted Cathryn from the downstairs lobby to Barry's office. Barry was all smiles, as was Cathryn. They grinned rather emptily at each other for a couple of seconds. Then Barry said, "Well, Cathryn, to what do we owe the pleasure of your company?"

"Oh, you know," Cathryn replied. "Life can be lonely in that chief executive suite. I needed to spend some time with one of my own kind."

"Yeah, tell me about it. You spend all day working your tail off and wonder if anyone around has a clue as to what you have to endure."

"My exact thoughts!"

This vapid exchange went on for a few more minutes. Finally, Barry decided to break the social inertia. "Okay, aside from camaraderie and exchanging the secret CEO handshake, perhaps you can tell me why you chose this moment to visit."

"I was thinking about a certain small proposal I recall your company submitted to us. Does that sound familiar?"

"Proposal . . . ah, yes. That does ring a bell." Barry felt proud of sounding like the king of cool, even though he felt anything but cool at the moment. "It sounds like we owe you a few more things. Would that be right?

"That would be right. How are those coming?"

"Well, in view of your time constraints, we have made this our number one priority. Those weren't exactly simple things you requested. I mean, we have all the information, but to pull them into a form fit for a board in the time frame of a few hours is causing some issues."

"Oh, what kind of issues?"

"Like giving you the margins on our latest projects when the data are still coming in. We are nearing the end of a quarter."

"They don't have to be fresh off the press," Cathryn spoke in a smooth, polished tone. "Just give us two or three representative projects from the past year."

"Okay." Barry was not sure he was feeling at all relieved. "But then there is the IP question. As you know, IP is hardly simple, and we would assume that would be part of the negotiation following the acceptance of the overall proposal."

Cathryn's smooth tone took on a slight cloying quality. "Give us some recommendations on the IP as a conversation starter, so we know what direction you are headed. We only need your best practical shot. We know time is short."

Barry started to feel relieved. "Well, that certainly makes sense. Given the professional reputations of our respective firms and the prospect of us having numerous opportunities to collaborate on business, that seems quite reasonable."

"Agreed. I trust you will figure out how to finesse as needed. But do make sure you have a really good answer on the Zinc contract termination. The board will really home in on that one."

Barry held his breath and tried not to show it. He exhaled slowly and said as noncommittally as possible, "That one's easy. I'm sure we'll have no problem giving you what you need."

"Good." She stood to leave. "Well, this has been fun, but now I must slog back to the salt mines."

She moved toward the door, Barry following close behind. As she crossed the threshold, she said over her shoulder, "Oh, one more thing. I thought it might be of interest to you that the reason why we are—" She stopped abruptly. Directly in her line of sight at Marjorie's desk stood Ray.

"Cathy! What are you doing here? Gee, you look great!"

"Cathy" froze. Her eyes widened in horror. She gulped, looked away, and stammered, "I–I'm here to talk to Barry . . ." Then, as if unable to stop herself, she added, "and not to you!"

The next thing that could be felt was the rush of air created by Cathryn tearing down the hall without so much as a glimpse in Barry's direction. Barry stood in stunned amazement and then hurried after her. He did not hurry fast enough. Cathryn made it to the elevator well ahead of him and dived through its serendipitously open door.

Ray let out an amused snort and ambled off to his next stop.

Barry stared down the hall in disbelief. Not knowing what else to do, he pushed back the hair that had just fallen into his eyes and walked back into his office. He made a beeline for the jellybean bowl, clutched it in his hands as he sank down onto the couch, and dug furiously for licorice jellybeans. Michael, however, had successfully mined all of them. That was too much!

"Marjorie!" he bellowed out the door. "Keep that snively nosed marketing kid out of here! He has no future at this company!" He turned around, satisfied that at least one thing was under control, and slammed his door shut.

After taking in Cathryn's rapid retreat, Marjorie buried herself into her computer screen. For the moment, it seemed safer to devote herself to her tenth chapter. She bent over the keyboard and added a line on how a young worker was summarily let go due to a jellybean infraction.

When the smoke cleared, she would catch up with Ray to find out what the deal was between him and Cathryn. She did not know where to begin with that one, but obviously he would, and that would be well worth giving up a couple of points on the tally sheet. *But what's going on with Barry? He was not in his usual take-charge self today. That Zinc thing seems to have opened up old wounds. I know losing it was tough, but I thought Barry had moved beyond it. It sure doesn't seem that way today. How come?*

Simon Stumbles into His Driver

Simon decided to take a break from Mexican food and his office— even he tired of the debris field. He walked down the street to the new Thai fusion restaurant. Actually, it was known in the hood as the "Thai confusion" restaurant due to the weird combinations of ingredients used by its aggressively inventive chef.

Today's offerings glowed with an unearthly green color and mysterious lumps of something floating in them. Simon did not care what was in there. He ordered a full-size meal with all the trimmings. He grabbed his recyclable container heaped with food and shuffled to the soda machine with his 30-ounce cup. Even the inventive Thai chef understood his customer market and the importance of diet sodas. While his cup filled, Simon checked out the restaurant clientele. He noticed Bernard Wu standing nearby. Bernard was a coder with whom he had worked in his early career days. Simon thought Bernard was okay as fellow coders go. Bernard had no deep affection for Simon, but at the same time held him in awe, as did most coders, for his legendary talent.

On a normal day, Simon would have paid little more than perfunctory attention to Bernard. Today was different, because Simon remembered Bernard worked at Zinc, or so he thought.

"Not any longer," Bernard said in response to Simon's question on how things were going at Zinc. "I left there a few weeks ago. I'm now over at Porter."

Simon fought to restrain his surprise and delight. Reach for the heavens, and they will provide.

"Porter . . ." he said slowly. "That's a fine establishment. So too, I thought, is Zinc. Porter must have worked hard to pry you out of there." Simon for all his antisocial behavior could also be quite coy.

"Well, yes and no." Bernard felt eager to talk with Simon. "Porter definitely gave me a good offer, but I was ready to move on."

"Really?" Simon spoke from the side of his mouth opposite the one that was sucking down his Diet Coke through a culvert-size straw. "How come?"

Given his awe of Simon, his table manners notwithstanding, Bernard could not keep himself from talking.

"That Mark guy," Simon looked puzzled, "the CEO. He hasn't a clue on how technology works. He talks a good game, but, man, he doesn't know the first thing about it. When you got fired, you actually were on to something. We couldn't make the Cloud connection work and without that your part of the project wouldn't work. Mark either didn't get it or didn't want to admit it. Either way, he decided the best solution was to let Arrow go rather than deal with it. A whole lot of valuable work went down the tube . . . Oh no, I probably have said too much. Please don't tell anybody I said anything!"

"Not to worry," Simon said nobly. "It stays here. Coders code. I appreciate you sharing. Good luck at Porter. It's a good spot."

The two men shook hands and left the shop.

Aside from the juicy bit of information he had now acquired, Simon was reminded of how much he loved being called "Simon, the Lion King of Coders."

Marco Confronts His Past and Finds a Way Forward

Marco stood in front of the bank of shiny lunchroom food machines. Behind him he could hear the hiss of the new espresso machine followed by a whoop of joy from an employee who had just succeeded in pulling the perfect cappuccino.

Coffee did not interest Marco right now. He was searching for comfort food to settle his stomach. He was not a foodie by nature. Nevertheless, today he had reached his upper limit of stress and did not know what else to do. Judging by the selection of vintage junk, his usual indifference to food was probably a good thing. He wondered how such a cross section of triglyceride-packed, food-colored, chemically enhanced items had escaped Barry's health-nut scrutiny.

The meeting with Barry about his calls to Porter was terrible. Why had he been such a coward? He could have asked Anthony for more information, but what if the guy got mad, told him he was stupid, or, worse, told others at Porter about Marco's question? Then where would Arrow be?

Then an old voice spoke up in his head. *Those are bad people. You will never succeed there. They don't want to know about the truth!* His dear old dad. His dad, whom he loved and respected. His dear old dad who did not understand him leaving the family fold to find his own path, something his dear old dad never did. Telling the truth at his former company had cost Marco his job. Now, to keep this job, he needed to find out the truth about Porter's interest in the Zinc termination. To do that he had to ask Anthony.

So what would it have taken for him to press Anthony, his old workmate from his former company, whether he knew more about the Porter deal with Arrow? He could tell Anthony he did not want him to say anything he didn't feel comfortable revealing, but if there was something he could share that would help the deal go forward, that would be great. What would be the harm in that?

Wait a minute. Why am I mincing? After all, it was Anthony who got me into trouble for talking about the altered fnancial reports that ended up costing me my job!

He knew Anthony had always felt bad about that. At the time, he hadn't thought about how sharing Marco's discovery on the financials might not turn out well for Marco. Anthony naïvely believed their manager's manager would side with Marco. How was he to know that the manager's manager was a close personal friend with their manager outside work?

Well, the manager's manager was tight with Marco and Anthony's manager. *The rest was history,* thought Marco with a scowl. *Okay. Now it is time for Anthony to do something good for me, and that "good" will be giving me some useful information!*

As he was finishing this inner dialogue, someone tapped him on the shoulder. There stood Claudia. He did not know her well. What he knew was that for some reason she did not give him the same hard time she gave others. She wasn't exactly respectful, but he had to admit that while she could be really caustic to the rest of the leadership team, she was civil to him.

Sometimes before meetings they talked with each other about their children who were of similar ages. Few on the leadership team had children or were inclined to talk about them. He wondered if anyone even knew Claudia had two children, much less how devoted she was to them. Whenever she talked about them, her face filled with warmth, that is, until someone else entered the room. Then she immediately quit talking.

He often wondered what made her afraid. Would it be so terrible if others saw her as human with, god forbid, human problems like the rest of us mortals? Power to her meant being a sealed vault of personal information.

"Hey, Marco," Claudia said in a light, airy voice. "Are you going to read all the food labels in those machines, or do you intend to make a choice?" She wore an amused smile.

"Oh, hi, Claudia." He was relieved to be shaken loose from his obsessing. "I guess translating the chemicals on these labels into their level of threat takes more work than I thought."

"I'd just close my eyes and punch a couple of buttons. Buying this stuff is rarely about the taste, which I suspect is the case for you at the moment."

He was taken aback by her uncharacteristic display of intuition. "Good advice." He punched two buttons and became the proud owner of a bag of Cheetos. *Could be worse,* he thought, *or could it?*

He nodded at her. She returned the nod. He left feeling oddly grateful for her compassionate moment. Time to call Anthony. He pulled his phone out of his pocket as he left the lunchroom.

Claudia Looks Inside and Starts to Unhook

Claudia walked back to her office feeling how nice it was to be ... nice, with no nasty edge attached. Her head was spinning with thought.

Marco is such a good guy who loves his children the way I love mine. Not only that, he has the courage to say it. Wouldn't it be great if my parents could do the same? I churn out perfect spreadsheets, receive this great industry award, and what is my reward? They are too busy seeing friends they see all the time to attend my award ceremony. What's with that? What is hiding behind all this perfection doing for me? Good question ...

And while I'm at it, what is the point of building a fence around myself all the time? I don't always know what to do, something I hate to admit, even to myself. Hell, I'm not sure when I am fairly sure I am right, especially when Barry or one of the others lobs some new wrinkle in my direction.

It seems like every project has a new product or some major twist in an existing product. I can't begin to guess how to fore-cast how many hours it will take, much less how much profit margin to put into the budget. If we didn't have to change so much to meet the market, we might actually compile an oper-ating history we could use for some credible future assump-tions. Instead, I have to wet my finger, stick it into the wind, and see which way it's blowing. I know the other execs are supposed to give me those assumptions, but isn't my job to validate them? Phew! Maybe I should go back to working in insurance. Well, maybe not.

Feeling that she was supposed to know everything scared Claudia to death.

She hesitated and sank back in her chair. Wow, what was she really saying? This was her career she was talking about. She stared up at her bookcase with all her business books and deal summaries. So many of them. She scanned the titles on the deal-book spines, one at a time. What was each about again? Then her eyes came to the end of the row and lighted on the most recent picture of her two children. They were not quite teenagers and so much fun. She couldn't help smiling broadly at that photo.

This morning while spooning his Cheerios, her eleven-year-old son asked her why she got so grouchy when she was about to leave for the office. They had been laughing about something their goofy cat had done. Then the clock struck eight, and it was time to go to work.

"Don't you like your job?" he asked. "You got an award for it, didn't you?"

How ironic that her children noticed her achievements, but not her parents. She answered him in a slow, tentative voice, "Well, yes, I did, and I do like my work."

"Then how come you look so grouchy when you are going there?" He was a serious eleven year old. He always had been that way.

"Oh, sometimes the people I work with can be difficult." Now wasn't that the pot calling the kettle black?

"I thought you liked them. You talk about them all the time and say nice things."

"Well, yes, I do. I guess it's only I don't like leaving you in the morning. That makes it hard to go out the door." That part was true.

Her son nodded and went back to his cereal.

Remembering this scene as she sat in her office, a horrible feeling struck her.

What if her children were in the work world, and she learned that they were behaving in the defended, obstructionist way she carried on? How would she react? No question but she would be incredibly upset. And yet, that is how she had been choosing to act, shielded from everyone else. Well, no, not everyone—mostly shielded from her judgmental, emotionally aloof parents.

Besides, what kind of role model was she giving her children—rigid, particular, and grouchy?

Oh, dear. All this energy being plowed into being perfect and for what? My coworkers resent it, I get evicted from the strategy discussions, and my parents couldn't care less. No, no, NO. My children need to know that "perfect" does not equal happiness. "To err is human." Isn't that what the English poet Alexander Pope said?

She had loved English literature in school. Besides, if she weren't so wound up defending herself all the time, she might actually discover something out there that was more satisfying, such as real human contact. That could even lead to other more interesting things. Maybe . . .

"No more," she bellowed across her empty office.

Her assistant heard these last words and rushed in. "Do you need something?" she asked nervously.

"Yes! But it is something I have to do myself. Thanks for checking."

It was time to pull out those reports Barry wanted for Porter and see if she could build a case.

Janey Seeks Advice from a Core Driver

Janey fidgeted nervously at her workstation. She was still smarting from her run-in with the condescending Nigel. How could he, an empty suit (even though he didn't wear suits) with nothing better than a firm handshake and shallow banter, diss her the way he did? Those Sales people never got the marketing thing. They thought that since the client contract got signed under their watch, no one else mattered in the process.

If Sales had been in charge during the Trash social debacle, Arrow would be stuck back in the dinosaur age selling to aged Baby Boomers who wanted only the stripped-down, lower-priced Arrow products. They didn't have the deep tech savvy her generation had with the fearless attitude toward trying new tools and devices. Marketing could bring Arrow into the modern age, linking it to the biggest upcoming demographic the market would see for the next forty years.

There are more of us Millennials than even the Baby Boomers who have monopolized the attention of the market for the past forty years, Janey concluded with a note of triumph and pride. Still, that did not solve her most immediate problem. She knew she had gone too far with Barry by accusing him of hogging the credit for things. While that might be true, saying it to him might not have been the wisest move. Now what?

She had texted her closest friend from college to exorcise her angst. She was savvy enough not to say anything about the substance of her interaction with Barry. She kept it more generic. The exchange went like this:

"OMG, I let my mouth shut off my brain at work today with a senior exec."
"Whaddya say?"
"NVM [never mind]. He doesn't get me."
"They never do, these old guys. What are you going to do?"
"Eat a bowl of pho and think."
"Pho! That's so yesterday!"
"Okay, what then?"

They went back and forth with food suggestions. After four or five ideas, Janey had enough. It was time to seek serious input. That meant calling her mom.

Both Janey's parents worked in professional firms. Her father was a structural engineer at a mid-sized local firm that specialized in designing bridges. Her mother served as the COO of a fast-growing, graphic design company. While her mother had a strong design aesthetic, she excelled at building and implementing systems. She loved it when the trains ran on time, so long as they did so as the result of a smart, elegant system.

Her parents had always been big champions of her as she grew. After attending the many childhood soccer games, school carnivals, and her brief flirtation with ballet, they now kept tabs on her career as an adult. She had always been an excellent student with a sense of flair that made her popular with both teachers and classmates.

She also was headstrong and driven to get what she wanted. An only child, she rarely had to compromise at the home front. This did not always serve her well in the world of work. She had gotten into numerous scrapes in her ten years of work, when in her zeal to deliver she had neglected to build buy-in along the way from key stakeholders. She had licked her wounds and learned what she could from each dust-up. The fine art of compromise did not come naturally to her, although she understood its importance. Whenever she forgot, she had her mother to remind her.

It was her mother Janey chose to call now. When she wanted unconditional positive regard, she called her father. As far as he was concerned, she could do no wrong. That was nice, but not terribly realistic she thought. When she needed to hear the hard facts of life, she called her mom.

"Mom!"

"Janey, dear. What's up?"

When you live in the same town as your parents, not much time passes between conversations. In fact, Janey and her mom spoke at least twice a week. Janey had already talked with her mom twice this week. The third time sent up her mom's antennae.

"I have a situation."

"What kind of situation?"

"Well, um, I . . ."

"You, 'well, um,' what, darling?" Her mom was growing impatient. She had a lot to do today and no time for twenty questions.

"I kinda, sort of . . ."

"Did what?"

"Insulted the CEO." Janey spoke quickly, as if the speed would reduce the impact of what she said.

"That's quite the 'what.' Okay, Janey. What happened? Talk to me." Her mother put extra emphasis on the word "talk."

Janey expected this direct approach. That is why she called her mother. It did not make it easy, but at least it was real, and might lead somewhere good even if the getting there was painful. After all, if she wanted to hide, she could have called her ever-loving dad. As much as she loved her dad, pleasing her high-achieving, determined mom meant more than anything.

"Okay, well, we are pitching this deal with a major new customer. Things seemed to be going okay, but then at the last minute the customer came back with a bunch of questions we have to answer by tonight."

"Why is that a problem? Customers usually don't ask for what they really want until the crunch is on."

"Yeah, well, I know that, but the CEO, he doesn't seem to be taking it seriously. He appears to be somewhere else."

"Do you know that for sure? Senior executives carry a lot in their brains that they don't share." Being a C-suite executive herself, Janey's mom knew this world all too well, something for which her daughter had deep respect. She was in awe of her mom's career and proud to be her daughter.

"Well, I ran into Arnie in the hall, and—"

"The junior sales exec?"

"Yeah, that's the one. Anyway, I saw him in the hall today, and I thought he said Barry, that's the CEO, wasn't paying much attention to the customer's requests."

"You 'thought he said'? Janey, how many times have we talked about not assuming? You don't know until you know. Never assume."

"Yeah, I know, I know. I understand that part. But actually, um, it gets worse. The problem is that I got mad at the CEO, telling him he wasn't paying attention to what the client wanted and, and—"

"And?" her mother wanted the punch line.

"I don't think he values me."

"What makes you think that?"

"Well, if he did, he would be paying attention to this deal I brought in."

"I don't follow how his not paying attention and your value are related. I imagine he's rather busy with a long list of things. He does run a company, you know."

"Sure, but this isn't your run-of-the-mill deal we're talking about. It's super important to the company's future."

"Okay. So you would like more evidence that he is working on it. Right?"

"Right."

"So why not ask him what he needs from you to answer the customer questions?" Her mom thought it was time to offer a minor suggestion.

"I was going to, but first I heard what Arnie said, and then I went to see Barry. While I was talking to him, Barry's eyes kept drifting to some spreadsheet on his computer for another deal. It pissed me off. If he thought I mattered, he would never have been so rude to me."

"Janey, again, what does that have to do with your value as a person?" Her mom was getting concerned. "All sorts of things could have been going on with Barry. You are not his only problem. You don't know what his situation currently is. It sounds like you were so consumed with how he viewed you, that you made no attempt to find out what was really going on for him."

Again, if she wanted coddling, she would have called dear old dad, Janey reminded herself. But she needed to take her medicine and her mom's words were not far from the truth. Might as well drop the other shoe.

"Okay, you're right. But, there is one more thing," she said.

Her mom was beginning to wonder if she wanted to hear this "one more thing," but being a parent meant listening to all sorts of things, however stressful.

"I said he wasn't paying attention, because I brought in the deal, and since he wasn't getting the credit, he wasn't interested."

Her mother did not respond right away. Finally, she said, "Oh dear. You said that?"

"Eeee . . . yes!" Janey felt embarrassed. "I know, I know! I shouldn't have, but he got me so mad! He comes across so condescendingly and I, I . . . I screwed up! Now what do I do?"

Her mother took a few moments to organize her thoughts. At last she replied in a voice gleaned from coaching many employees. "Well, what's done is done. Now what do you think would be a good next step?"

"Well, I think I'd better figure out where things really are on the customer's questions," Janey said, pulling from her strategic chops.

"That's a good start." Her mom wanted to reinforce a constructive route and avert the train wreck her daughter was in the process of causing. "It would be good to base things on fact rather than emotions. It also sounds like you might have been personalizing whatever he said. Was he really criticizing you or perhaps reacting to a broader situation?"

How often had Janey heard that? It wasn't that emotions did not matter, her mother had told her, but you need to know where to put them. And, yes, she heard Barry questioning her value, rather than him expressing exasperation with the situation. Her mother interrupted her rumination.

"Okay, and then what?" Her mother liked to be results oriented. Janey had mixed feelings about that orientation, but she understood its relevance in this situation.

"I have to apologize to Barry."

"Yes. That's what smart executives do. If for no other reason than it gives room to others to do the same."

"Okay. Got it. Thanks, Mom, for being there."

"Always. You're worth it!"

They hung up. Armed with a plan, Janey was ready to face the scary prospect of going back to Barry to set things right. It would make her mother, and her, extremely proud.

Chapter 4: Late Afternoon—
The Arrow Leadership Team Unites

Barry Takes Stock and Unearths His Core Driver

Barry felt depressed. He brooded in his chair after the unseemly departure of Cathryn. His mind turned over many thoughts. *Why is this all so hard? So much emotionality from so many people! What's going on here? I can't get anyone to do anything! Claudia thinks I disdain accurate data. Janelle assumes I don't understand a thing about legal complexities. Nigel thinks my quest for answering client questions is a big time waster. Marco worries that I am too nosy about what goes on outside this company. Janey accuses me of hogging all the credit. Arnie sees me as not paying attention. Simon the silent . . . who knows?*

Then he thought about what had just happened outside his office.

And what is the deal with Cathryn and Ray? What in the world was that about? The things I have to take into account! I guess I heard they were in high school together. Don't tell me they dated! Or did they? Improbable pairs seem to be the hallmark of high school dating. But does that mean that to be successful in business I have to know people's social history? Is there any limit to what I am supposed to know?

A small voice from somewhere within said, "No." That depressed him even more.

Then there was the phone call earlier that day from Bill Morely.

"Barry, my man! How are things?" asked his lawyer friend in a sonorous voice.

"Uh, okay, I guess." Somehow he could never fake it with Bill.

"Uh-huh. That strikes me as rather qualified. You want to tell me what's going on?"

"Nothing, that's what." In saying this, Barry moved closer to telling the truth than he had all day. He went on to talk about the Porter deadline and the questions Arrow had to answer. When he got to the Zinc question, Bill interrupted.

"What do you mean, you don't know what happened there? Didn't you go talk to Mark Miller? Even if he told you only a little, you would have learned something."

Barry cringed. "Well, Mark is not exactly the most trustworthy of folks. I have only met him a couple of times at industry events and once again when we closed the Zinc deal. What I hear is that you never know how he will react. He can be your best friend one day and then the next day he has badmouthed you all over town. I decided it wasn't worth it."

"I see. Well, putting aside for now the question of why you didn't dig further into his modus operandi, I can't help believing somebody at Zinc, besides Mark, knows what happened. Did you ask your people to work their underground? Coders love to kibitz with one another in the name of pure engineering."

"My guys did do a little nosing around and came up empty. Anyway, I decided we were better off directing our energy to the Excelsior project you and I discussed over dinner."

"Digital filing for lawyers?"

"Well, yeah, isn't that what we were talking about?" Bill's lack of enthusiasm surprised him.

"Well, yes, and it's not a terrible idea. However, right now I'd say the Porter deal is going to do a whole lot more for your company than any law-related project. It also, I'd venture to say, would do more for you than the rarefied market of techies the Zinc product would have served. If you want that Porter deal, I think you are stuck uncovering what happened with Zinc, uncomfortable as that might be for you."

Barry squirmed in his chair. Even thinking about the Zinc termination still filled him with anxiety. Talking with Mark was a risky proposition, and he wasn't sure where else to go. He also felt ashamed for losing that deal. Failure was never an option where he grew up, and Zinc definitely felt like a big failure to him. Bill, as usual, had good advice. He had to solve the mystery of what happened with Zinc if he wanted to win the Porter deal. It seemed like Cathryn was about to tell him something relevant to that before the unfortunate run-in with Ray, whatever that was about.

Barry and Bill exchanged a few closing words and hung up. Barry went back to thinking about Zinc and why it was so stressful to dig into what happened there.

It was getting late in the day. Barry studied the angle of the sun as it dipped on the horizon, now shining through rather than over the trees. The late afternoon light reminded him of visiting his father, the man who was never at home except to grab a quick dinner and arrange his weekend golf games.

He remembered that while growing up sometimes his mother would be out at some event after school and he, either alone or with his brother, would go hang out at their father's office until their mother would pick them up. They would sit in the chairs in the outer office opposite his father's assistant. She was nice to them.

Sometimes when Barry went alone, he was allowed to wait inside his father's office. He'd sit in the corner pretending to read his book when really he was watching his father. His father was almost always on the telephone. He sat in his chair or stood up and paced like a caged tiger while he made his point to someone at the other end of the line. Between calls he checked something on a pad of paper he kept on his desk, grumbled, then made another phone call. Barry knew not to say anything. His father did not tolerate failure, in himself or in anyone else. Each detail had to be managed. He ground away on that phone until he got what he wanted. Then he let out a satisfied grunt and dialed the phone for the next conquest.

Barry followed his father's every move. Even as a boy, however, he was struck by how alone his father seemed. His mother and father were still married. They appeared to have their understandings. She had her life. He had his. Barry had never wanted either of theirs. He and his younger brother felt like social accessories. Their parents proudly displayed family photos on their respective desks—his mother's desk at home and his father's desk at his office. Beyond that, what was the connection?

Barry had sworn that he would not grow up like that man on the phone, pacing in his office or silently loading his golf clubs into the freshly washed car. That life of perfection. What happiness did that bring? In his own life, Barry had decided he would have connection, dealing with the imperfect state of the world as it was, rather than what it was not. He would know why he was there and who was there with him.

So how had he done on that?

He thought first about how he had handled, or, rather, not handled the loss of the Zinc deal. It shocked and scared him. He thought they had done everything right, like the good book (that is, his father) said. When they were unceremoniously turned out, he told himself the story that Zinc was a bad customer. With the arrogant Mark Miller at the helm, that was an easy escape. However, they had been dismissed when he thought things had smoothed out. Sure, they had a rough start and some shaky intervals when his team had more questions than their team had answers. But if the chemistry between the teams was the issue, why choose a time of peace rather than war to sever the alliance?

But what if he dug into the Zinc deal and found out Arrow did something wrong? What then? Mark could make his life utterly miserable in the market. But, hadn't he done that already by firing Arrow? Why else would Porter, Inc., be asking about that project? So what had he done? Disengaged and hidden in the Excelsior project, a brand new initiative with no baggage to defend. Well, he might have thought he escaped the pain of reality, but apparently Porter did not agree. So much for connecting to the world as it really was.

He then turned his mind to his leadership team, the people with whom he should be connected to solve the Zinc problem.

He thought first about Arnie—youngish, earnest Arnie. He had the right intentions but was so colossally conflict averse. How in the world could he convince others to do things that were hard, or even easy for that matter? It had not helped that Barry had sent him off like a lamb to the slaughter to gather all that information for Porter, when he, of all people, knew what barriers would be thrown up in front of him. Barriers, not incidentally, that Barry allowed to be raised with his own disengaged leadership.

Then there was Janey—another earnest young person. She had worked hard and brought a lot to the company. She could be really annoying, no doubt. That crack about him taking the credit. Did she have to personalize so much? She needed major feedback on that score. And who was going to give her that? Well, obviously, her manager. And her manager was . . . uh-huh . . .

Janelle, the queen of perfection and micromanagement. Wow, he didn't know how she had grown up, but that obsessive attention to detail must have served some purpose. *At one level I have to feel sorry for her,* sighed Barry. *Besides, who am I to criticize on the perfection front? Perhaps a little empathy is in order?*

Claudia. Ohhh. She could be so ascendant and petty. Like Janelle, she always had to be right and never gave an inch. Everything also had to be perfect for her, and perfect, to Claudia, meant her way or the highway. Worse, like Janey, she was always personalizing, taking any feedback as an assault on her self-worth. On the other hand, when something needed to be done, she would be the first to stay late. She knew her stuff and would keep everything in order, which is not a bad thing. She did have a nasty habit of playing that relationship with the chair of the board of director's card. Well, they would have to deal with that. That was reality, and politics are politics. Besides, that relationship with the chair could be useful.

Then there was Marco, his disciplined and honorable head of Operations. Marco had at least tried to talk with his former colleague who was now at Porter, and what had Barry done when Marco proceeded cautiously? He criticized him for not doing enough instead of encouraging him to do more.

Nigel—glib, disengaged, and only accountable if others were in there with him. Not a great profile. At the same time, there was something that lay beneath. Sometimes when he returned from one of his many road trips, he looked unusually weary. His behavior felt more like an emotional override rather than genuine enthusiasm. Barry did not know what else was going on in Nigel's life, but he sensed that something was pulling him down. He was grateful for Nigel's great loyalty with his willingness to stay on the road and keep customers happy. Life could be worse than that. Maybe he needed a bit more appreciation. What, exactly, was beneath? It sure would be good to know.

And speaking of appreciation, how about Simon—brilliant, recalcitrant, slobby Simon? If ever there were a person on whom Barry could rely for coming through, it was Simon. What would Arrow have done in the Trash debacle had it not been for Simon? *Did I tell him that?* wondered Barry. He winced when he realized he wasn't sure, and the truth was "probably not." And who among the coder empire would know more about what went on there than Simon? Why had he not pushed Simon to infiltrate that empire and find out what happened with Zinc? Why indeed? Maybe because Simon's combination of being scary, smart, and grumpy intimidated Barry. Well, that was one for Barry's next coaching session.

So far his balance sheet on connections with his leadership team was not looking good. *Here we are in this crucial Porter deal with the CEO showing up, and I can't even be sure I can motivate my own people to deliver. Quelle catastrophe! Okay, this makes me nervous and crazy, but it is time to change this scene. I will connect. I will make this work. We are not making any progress on figuring out this Zinc thing and I need this team to do that. I have been busy avoiding inconvenient truths, whatever they are, and gutless! Time to get real and enter into the present to uncover what we really need to know about Zinc.*

He opened his office door and called for Marjorie. "Time for a meeting, Marjorie. Time to lay out all the chips. I need the leadership team here in fifteen minutes . . . please." He added the "please," realizing he had not done well with Marjorie either. He gave her a wan smile, stretched his arms widely, and went back into his office to move the chairs into an arrangement more conducive to conversation.

The Arrow Team Solves the Zinc Mystery

Reminiscent of the final drawing-room scene in an Agatha Christie murder mystery, the members of the Arrow leadership team assembled in Barry's office. Claudia seated herself in his best guest chair. Barry watched her and wondered whether Arrow needed to add a line item to its budget for her sedan chair.

He resisted going further down that line of thinking, reminding himself that this was a time of connecting, not disconnecting.

Nigel settled back into his favorite spot on the couch. This time he kept his feet off the coffee table. Janelle sat carefully upright in the second guest chair. Janey brought in a chair from Marjorie's space and placed it as far from Nigel as physically possible without invading Barry's personal space. She put on her most professional, team-player face. Marco leaned against the wall and remained standing, as he generally preferred to do. Arnie sat on the floor against the wall. He was used to it. Simon arrived last, plunking his pinecone form heavily onto the other end of the couch. He briefly considered the jellybean bowl, but the Thai confusion lunch had taken its toll on his intestines. He decided to take a brief break from food.

Barry sat on the edge of his desk, cleared his throat, and began.

"Thank you for coming on such short notice, but I'm sure you all know we have a situation here. We are close to winning the Porter deal, and close to losing it. And lose it we will if we don't cross this last hurdle and answer the five questions the Porter team has asked." Heads nodded, but the room remained quiet.

"Everybody here has been asked to help answer those questions. I know they call for information that requires a close review of our internal data, some of which is not available. Other information needs to have proper legal vetting so that we don't paint ourselves into a corner we later find ourselves not liking. All of this I understand."

"What I didn't understand, at least at first, is why we are not doing a better job of pulling together to make this happen. After all, unless I'm wrong, we all care about winning this Porter deal."

He looked around. Heads nodded again, except for Simon who seemed preoccupied with examining his nails as if seeing them for the first time.

Barry went on with his opening remarks. "Now, I know everyone in this room is capable of delivering the goods. That isn't the issue. What I don't know is how to move you beyond whatever is standing in the way of you delivering what we need on this Porter deal.

"To get us past this impasse, I decided to start by doing a little soul searching about my own behavior. So, this afternoon I spent some time peering into various dark personal corners. Not easy to do, but it's helped me to come up with a few ideas. I'd like to share them with you on the hope they might point us in a more positive direction."

Barry did not wait for a reaction. This would be hard enough without feedback, good or bad.

"First, I think it would be a whole lot easier for you to deliver if I actually gave you the serious support each of you deserves. I know I get buried in my own projects and when you come to me asking for help, I am often only half there. My mind is on the business, for sure, but it's not on the specific aspect of the business each of you brings to me. That's wrong. How can I ask you to engage if I don't?

"Second, instead of giving you constructive feedback on what you do, I pick at it, demand more without listening to where you are going or encouraging you for the good things you are doing. That's got to change.

"Third, I could quit taking pot shots to avoid hearing all you have to say.

"Fourth . . . Well, I could go on with my list of leadership sins, but we don't have enough time for that right now." He looked around at the group with a self-effacing smile.

"So, if you don't mind, I'd like to skip to what I need most to say. It's something I don't have a lot of practice saying, but here goes." He hesitated, and then said, "I'm sorry."

The team members eyed one another not knowing how to react. The rest of the list was interesting but this last thing? Barry showing his flank like that? The room remained eerily quiet, as every person processed what Barry had said.

"'Sorry,' you ask? Yes, sorry for not paying better attention to what each of you has done and is trying to do for our organization. You are all here because you are remarkable at what you do. That you choose to do it here is something for which I am deeply grateful. Thank you. Thank you, all, for everything that you do and for being part of this company."

Some in the room started to move their heads slowly up and down. A couple of them gave close-lipped smiles.

"Later, after we get through this Porter issue, I want to spend time with each of you to find out how I can do a much better job of supporting you. Today, we have a problem where time is of the essence. That's the expression they use in law, isn't it, Janelle?"

"Yes."

"So might we put our heads together to figure out how to produce a winning package of answers to get over to Porter by six?"

The words "yes" and "sure" could be heard around the room.

Barry went on to talk about his visit with Cathryn, at least up until her hasty departure. After Barry described Cathryn's willingness to be pragmatic and her suggestions, the group talked through the first four questions and came up with a game plan.

They were about to break camp, when Arnie piped up. He had been watching the room and noticing a lot of looking up, down, and all around after the first four questions were addressed. Enough already. What Porter really wanted was an answer to the Zinc question. The rest was pure garnish.

He rose from the floor where he had been sitting and in a strong, clear voice said, "Barry, what about the Zinc question?"

"Yes, Arnie. Thanks for remembering that nasty bit," Barry answered with a pained smile.

"Yes, Arnie. Nice timing," Nigel sneered. Arnie paid no attention to him.

Janelle angrily whipped her head around toward Nigel. "Oh, quit it, Nigel. What would you know about timing? You live out there on the road with no timing but your own!"

"What would you know about what happens to me on the road? You don't know anything." Nigel was still feeling the ache of his last visit home, although he was not about to share that with anyone.

Janelle started to say, "Well, and whose fault is that?" when she caught herself. She really didn't have any idea of what he was talking about, except that he was right. She did not know what he was out there doing. Had she ever bothered asking him about it?

"You're right. I'm sorry." Her words were almost inaudible, but nevertheless clear. She opened her mouth to add something but quickly closed it again when she saw Barry raise his hand.

"Obviously, you two have something to discuss, but not right this moment. We can deal with our internal politics later . . . and we should. For now, allow me to continue. Nigel and I talked about the Zinc question. He is going to put together an explanatory note that emphasizes our philosophy and track record of superior customer service. Janey, I expect you to work with Nigel on that."

Janey replied, "Of course."

Barry went on. "We were unable to deliver to Zinc. We were not a good fit with its corporate culture, and that we might also need to explain."

While he was saying this, his eyes traveled over to Simon whose face remained impassive. *I will wind back to him as soon as the others have left,* Barry thought. *If he knows something, it is unlikely he will say anything with the rest of the team around.* Barry turned his attention back to the rest of the room, "How does that sound to everyone?"

Most of them nodded their heads. Janelle did not. Her walk back to the office after seeing Cathryn at the health club got her thinking. She wondered what was going on with Porter and that intense woman. She also thought about what was going on with her own intensity that refused to stick her neck out to help people who mattered to her. Her conversation earlier that day with Claudia about how she brought her family issues into the workplace stuck with her. She didn't know yet what to do with it, but there definitely was something to it. Here was a chance to say something to people who mattered to her.

"I think that is a good strategic approach. But you know, I think there is more to it than that." Janelle went on to explain how she periodically worked out in the health club at the same time as Cathryn, and how Cathryn talked with her trainer about a wide range of topics besides fitness.

"One of the things that keeps coming up is mention of this guy, Mark. I thought at first he was a boyfriend of hers, but the more I heard, the more I started to think that it was someone in business. Then I wondered, given this Zinc question, whether the Mark she is talking about is Mark Miller, the CEO of Zinc."

"Wow," said Barry. "Now that is interesting. What does she say about him?"

"It's rather nonspecific, but there seems to be some kind of competitive thing going on between them."

Nigel was still thinking about Janelle's earlier surprise apology and was not sure where to go with that. For the present, with the Porter commission firmly in mind, he decided to rejoin the group and the conversation. "Why would that be? They compete for different customers."

"That's true, but, call it women's intuition or whatever you want," Janelle smiled wryly. "She does not like that guy and wants to beat him at something."

"I hate to ask," Barry said, thinking of the recent run-in between Cathryn and Ray, "but did Cathryn and Mark ever date each other?"

"No!" Janelle and Claudia said in unison.

Then Claudia said, "It's a little-known fact, but it happens to be true, that women actually compete for things beyond men."

"Claudia . . ." said Barry raising his eyebrows at her in an appeal to her better self.

Claudia avoided his look. "Okay, okay."

Janelle continued, "No, as far as I know, they never dated." Then in response to the puzzled looks in the room, "It's a small town and even smaller when you are single and work in the same industry. I think they actually went to business school together. Both were ace students, and you still hear about how outstanding both of them were in school. Maybe a rivalry was born there."

Suddenly Marco's voice could be heard. "I learned a similar thing." Everyone gaped at him in surprise. He almost never talked in leadership team meetings. "My friend, Anthony, over at Porter said he doesn't know exactly what it is, but there is for sure something weird between Cathryn and Mark that goes way back to business school, and it's causing serious pressure to get our deal done."

"Well, given that, I'd say we better hurry up and find the pressure point. Good sleuthing, you two. Thank you," Barry said. "I'll poke around on this in the next hour. In the meantime, if anyone else learns something more, let me know. By the way, Janelle, do we pay your health club fees? If not, we should."

"I can sign up for that." Claudia saw this as a good moment to join forces.

Barry thanked the group and adjourned the meeting.

The team members jumped to their feet to go to work on their Porter response. That is, except Simon. As if he had heard Barry's inner thoughts, he remained seated until the last person left the room. Barry looked over at him, wondering what was going on in his mind. He had tremendous respect for Simon's big brain and knew that it never had anything in it that was not interesting, although sometimes it might be disgusting or bizarre.

"What is it, Simon? You have that look on your face."

Simon had the look of the Lion King of Coders. He was fairly sure he had the missing piece. He said nothing for a moment, soaking up the pleasure of his power in the room. Then he spoke. "Well, it seems there is a bit of a problem over in the Zinc shop. A little bird told me that there appears to be some technical difficulties with its platform." He had the amused expression of someone used to others not being as smart as he was.

Barry got up and closed the door. He settled down into the guest chair opposite Simon, leaned forward, and said, "Go on."

"Apparently, when we were working for them, we were on the brink of discovering that the foundation of their platform was not strong enough to support the movement of their new whizz-bang, ultra-esoteric functionality to the Cloud."

"Huh?" Barry worked to take this in. "What do you mean? How could we possibly have succeeded on that project without them having a solid foundation? We were supposed to create a program that worked with a system they said was Cloud-ready."

"Indeed, and that's what my guys were in the process of uncovering. Rather embarrassing, I'd say. It gets worse. It seems that their CEO knows nothing about technology and didn't even know how to ask the right questions to turn things around. He heard the squawking of his coders and threw us under the bus before it got out that they don't know what they're doing over there."

"Whaaaa? He doesn't know tech? What are you talking about?"

Simon explained.

"How's it possible he made it this far in the business?" Barry asked.

"Oh, it's possible if you ask enough questions and play your political cards right. General smarts have their place. Then again, there's that expertise thing—"

"It definitely helps," Barry agreed, still processing this new information about Zinc. "No wonder we had to go. Our people would have noticed the emperor had no clothes. So, why didn't you tell me this before . . . oh, never mind. And so the only way Mark could save face and protect his reputation, phony as it is, would be for him to remove us before we knew enough to hurt his self-view, not to mention the view of others."

"A-yup."

"But, where does all this stuff with Cathryn fit in?"

"That I don't know, but I have my suspicions." Simon paused, then took on an authoritative manner. "As you might recall, our proposed contract with Porter involves putting their offerings into the Cloud. I think Cathryn is gunning to invade Mark's space before he gets his act together. Those old business school rivalries can run deep, you know, and displacing Zinc could be an incredibly shrewd move, not to mention a nice diversification for Porter, which, by the way, is overdue."

Simon finished his short speech and sat back deep into the couch, a satisfied grin on his face.

Barry blew out a long gust of air. "So, what does Cathryn get from learning why Zinc got rid of us?"

"She probably wants to make sure she's backing the right horse to ride past Zinc's position. Not unreasonable, when you think about it."

Barry nodded slowly as he worked to digest all of what Simon was telling him.

Simon continued, "From what I have heard about her, I would wager that Cathryn has already figured out what happened. But she has to demonstrate to her board that she did her due diligence on us."

"Okay, if you are right, what do we do about this?"

"Step around the competitive cow pies, I'd say. Our job is to make the large opportunity in the Cloud happen for Porter. That is, as you know, what they asked us to do, and, coincidentally, what we actually do."

"But Zinc will never hire us again."

"It's not going to, anyway, at least as long as Mark is there. Believe me, we also learned nothing competitively useful about the company that would prevent us from working for Porter."

Barry nodded in assent. He would talk with Janelle to make sure. In the meantime, his thoughts were on closing the Porter deal.

"I wonder if it would be good to propose to Cathryn that I attend her board meeting tonight to answer the director's questions in person."

"I like it," Simon said in a rare display of enthusiasm. "I imagine she will too. I can give you a hand with the technology prep part."

"Excellent." Barry then threw open his office door. "Marjorie?"

Marjorie was an inch outside the door. "Marjorie, will you please call Cathryn's office and get Ms. Porter on the line? I want to discuss tonight's meeting with her.

"Yes, I know, I mean, I know the number," Marjorie said, hastily trying to cover her eavesdropping tracks.

Barry chuckled and turned back to Simon. "Simon, have I ever told you how incredible you are?"

"Not recently."

"Well, Simon, you are amazing." He leaned over to shake Simon's hand. "Thank you, Simon, for being you."

"Guess I'm stuck with that." Simon actually smiled. "By the way, when the Porter storm has blown over, we might want to talk about that Excelsior project . . ."

Epilogue
March, Two Years Later

Marjorie surveyed the large conference room, pleased with her work. All stood in readiness for the second anniversary party of the Arrow/Porter project. She thought back two years to that day when it looked like the Arrow leadership team members would rather stay stubbornly locked in their refusal to face the facts of life about Zinc and themselves than win a deal that had since then reaped major dividends.

She smiled as she remembered the leadership team meeting breaking up near the end of that day. First, she saw Claudia walking out and smiling as she talked with Marco about how to give him better numbers. Next came Janelle taking Arnie's elbow and apologizing, actually apologizing, for being so obstinate about his request for intellectual property terms, or something like that. They sped down the hall together in search of the "right language," she thought she heard Janelle say. Nigel and Janey flew by, talking a blue streak about writing up some big piece on the "platinum" (Marjorie was sure she heard the word "platinum") grade client service Arrow offered its customers.

Then things got kind of quiet, as Simon remained in Barry's office and Barry shut the door. *I hated that,* thought Marjorie. Mercifully, the door was not that thick. It sounded like Simon had picked up some intelligence that maybe the great Mark Miller wasn't so great. Perhaps that's why not long after Arrow won the Porter deal, Mark's board fired him. *I never met him, but according to Ray, and once in a while Ray is right, Mark was a world-class jerk.*

When that closed door finally opened (with me a little close to it—how embarrassing), I had to arrange for Barry to go over to the Porter board meeting to answer those five questions. The Porter team was fine with that, although I heard Cathryn was a bit off her feed after some meeting she had in the middle of the afternoon. I suspect that meeting was the unplanned one with Ray. I caught up with him later and got the scoop on Cathryn and him. Now that was funny. Totally worth the loss of a couple of tally sheet points and definitely went into my book, cleverly disguised, I think. I'll know soon. My agent left a message today saying she had good news and needed a major edit. Hmm.

Anyway, for the next hour, members of the leadership team trotted in and out of Barry's office proffering materials for his Porter meeting. Finally, Barry was set to go, and who went with him? Simon. Well, there is no one more expert than Simon in explaining the virtues of technology. It's funny. When he finally stepped out of his disengaged, cynical shell, he took on this almost warm, homey approach, as if he was sitting in your kitchen eating cookies and merely passing the time.

Well, it worked. Apparently, the Porter board really liked what Barry and Simon had to say. The directors gave our deal a thumbs-up. Oh, yes, and then, according to Barry when we chatted later, Cathryn and Simon got into some animated geek chat. Since then, they have become supreme buds. They're not dating, thank heavens, but it has brought out the better part of Simon. He is a whole lot less prickly these days. I hear he is even mentoring young techies in town through a nonprofit association. That started soon after Barry promoted him to senior vice president. Well, he is talented.

The next day, Janey apologized to Barry for accusing him of taking the credit. Barry must have accepted, because after she said she wanted to learn more about the business, she ended up with the role as his right hand. I couldn't listen to that conversation, finding it rather unbearable. Anyway, he likes her most of the time now. She is a quick study and at least catches herself before her entitled foot swings into her mouth.

Nigel and Janelle must have had some kind of a conversation later on. From time to time I now hear them walking by, comparing notes about the care and feeding of dysfunctional families. Rumor has it that Nigel actually vetted the terms of a big sale with Janelle before agreeing to them with the customer. It was a small step for the rest of us, but a big one for Nigel. He and Barry seem to be talking more, and the dialogue sounds less glib and superficial. He might yet land in my book.

Janelle hired an executive coach to work with her controlling stuff. Joyce tells me that she still requires birthday parties to start and end on time, but she has cut back overall on the micro-management. She even solicits suggestions these days.

Marco received a big award this January for being a leader in technical operations for our local tech industry. He really stretched these past couple of years and came up with some new innovative approaches to customer service. His father threw a big family party to celebrate the award. While I hear he could not resist saying at the party how he missed having his son in the trucking business, he had a brilliant smile on his face as he told the gathering about how proud he was of his son for "being his own man."

Arnie got his own sales region and is knocking it out of the park. He is a bit pushier these days, but he does it in such a pleasant, principled way. It's good to see him move out of Nigel's shadow. Nigel seems okay with that. Once in a while I see Arnie slip into his old habit of letting people fob him off. I like to remind him that he is more likely to get what he wants if he actually asks for it. He seems to appreciate me doing that.

Claudia brought her daughter into the office for a "Take Your Daughter to Work" event and grinned like a Cheshire cat all day. She has been shadowing Marco and a couple of the engineers to understand the business better. She says with a weird laugh, "It makes me better at my numbers." She still has her rigid moments. Barry is learning to assure her that she is smart and worthy. That seems to help her ease up.

Barry still has his edge. He and the rest of us need that, after all. At the same time, he quit pursuing that Excelsior project. Simon finally sat him down and explained that trying to sell technology to the legal community would prove to be a long, maddening process. Janelle reluctantly agreed with Simon. Barry must have heard them, because he instantly plowed into other new things, including expansion of the platform created by the Porter deal. Porter did make Arrow a whole lot cooler in the market.

Barry now does this "411 chat" at his monthly leadership team meetings. That's when they put their heads together to talk about what they have heard and what rumors they need to confirm about the tech community products, talent, ownership, you name it. No more blindsiding by the likes of Zinc. The team members seem to like that meeting. A blast of energy comes out of that room, especially when I hear the clicking of jellybeans coming out of the sacred bowl. With or without jellybeans, there is no doubt our success rate has risen on closing deals.

Barry finally bought his wife her new car on the promise that he would never have to drive it. I'm not sure how that turned out, as I am fairly sure I saw it sitting at the far corner of our parking lot a couple of weeks ago.

It sounds like Cathryn recovered from her visit to our office. According to my sources, she is now dating a nice divorced guy whose daughter plays on Ray's soccer team. Ray and Cathryn don't exactly converse at games, but I understand she will show up and at least say hello to him. Ray generally does not notice, I hear. He is usually too busy making sure his girls play great soccer.

Part 4

THE JOURNEY OF NOT KNOWING MODEL

The Core Four

THE JOURNEY OF Not Knowing model has four components known as the Core Four. All the components revolve around the relationship between leadership and the unknown.

The Core Four are

1. *Bigger Bets:* Strategic new ideas that lie in the unknown and propel you to create a stronger, more successful organization.

2. *The Risks of the Unknown:* The risks you encounter when you move into the unfamiliar world of the unknown to pursue bigger bets.

3. *Hooks:* Defensive behaviors that give you short-term relief from the discomfort of the risks of the unknown, but will prevent you from reaching your bigger bets.

4. *Drivers:* Your personal motivators that provide fuel to move you through the discomfort from the risks of the unknown toward achieving bigger bets.

The story about the day in the life of Arrow, Inc., highlighted the perils and opportunities of crossing from what was known into the unknown. It demonstrated the waste caused by its leaders refusing to deal with what they either did not know or did not want to know about what was really going on in their business and within themselves. The avoidance of what Arrow team members did not know had the potential to cost them the Porter project, a major bigger bet that would move Arrow into a larger and trendier customer market.

When the Arrow leadership team was willing to face that it did not know what happened with Zinc and what got in the way of the team members dealing constructively with each other, it was able to pull together into a united effort to win the Porter deal. Each character navigated his or her own course. To do that, they had to take their own journeys, working through their respective hooks and resistances to exploring the unknown. Ultimately they overcame their avoidance of the scariness of what they did not know by discovering personal drivers. Their drivers enabled them to confront the discomfort masked by their hooks and pursue the Porter bigger bet.

Each element of the Core Four is illustrated in the Arrow story.

1. Bigger Bets

A bigger bet is a new strategic idea that lifts the organization into the future by making it better. It can touch any facet of business, such as strategic positioning in the market, a new approach to execution, corporate culture, or a structure that facilitates smarter work. It does not have to be radical or huge. It does have to be better than what is directly in front of you to leverage the possibilities of the emerging future and compel others to act.

The bigger bet for Arrow was to win the Porter contract, which had the potential to increase its customer base significantly by entry into the much broader market served by Porter.

2. The Risks of the Unknown

Success as a leader requires embracing the unknown. Only by seeking out new ideas can leaders develop smart growth strategies for their organizations. By their nature, new ideas are untested, hence their outcomes are unknown. That uncertainty makes them uncomfortable.

The unknown falls into two categories: the external unknown and the internal unknown.

The External Unknown includes the wide universe of people and events that can have an impact on your business—economic trends, global politics, social evolution, technology, and changing demographics. In the twenty-first-century, global, 24/7, hyper-connected world, people and events change every second of every day. Many of these changes can have an impact on organizational strategy, even for locally based businesses. Talent, capital, and products flow from every part of the globe, connected by the fast, instant, and enormous capacity of digital conduits. Figuring out everything you need to know is impossible. However, to not reach out and learn what you can might prove fatal to your ability to build a future.

Arrow ignored the reason for Zinc's termination and, by doing so, not only risked losing the Porter opportunity, but also missed seeing the shift in competitive positioning in the market represented by Porter deciding to go after the space targeted by Zinc.

The Internal Unknown is what you do not know about yourself that could prevent you from connecting effectively with people and things. To gain the trust of others to inspire their best ideas and work, you need to be clear about who you are and what you want. If you do not know yourself, what moves you forward and what holds you back, you will be unable to convince others to join you on the adventure of finding and trying out new ideas.

To see clearly outside yourself requires seeing clearly what is inside. Self-awareness is power. It surfaces who you uniquely are, what values you hold dear, and the dreams you want to realize. While you will never know everything about yourself, your willingness to see yourself as you are, not as you should be, provides you with the authenticity that allows followers to connect to you and your dreams for making things better.

Throughout the Arrow story, all the leadership team members stumbled along with their lack of awareness about their defensive behaviors and the significant negative impact they had on solving the Porter challenge.

3. Hooks

Hooks are defensive behaviors that lessen the discomfort of not knowing but take us off the pathway toward achieving bigger bets. There are many hooks. The ten most common hooks fall into three thematic buckets: operational hooks, individual contributor hooks, and invisibility hooks.

Operational Hooks: The road to success for a leader is long and paved with uncertainty. The underlying unknown is, "Will this idea work?" Operational hooks are behaviors that provide immediate feedback to subdue the anxiety of waiting for an unknown result. They give leaders a "Do Do Do" mindset. Leaders caught by these hooks invest energy in achieving tasks that yield instant feedback on how the bigger bet might play. Unfortunately, concentrating on tactical maneuvers erects a barrier to strategic thinking and thwarts attaining the bigger bet.

The operational hooks are

- micromanagement
- perfectionism
- conflict avoidance
- codependence

Individual Contributor Hooks: These are the "Me, Me, Me" hooks. The underlying unknown is, "What is my value?" These hooks appear when leaders think in terms of their individual success rather than that of the broader enterprise. The crux of leadership is leveraging the talents of others. To achieve that, a leader has to navigate through the unpredictability and messiness of humans. A leader's preoccupation with personal concerns, rather than the interests of others, makes it hard to connect with people to gain their alignment with bigger bets.

Not only does the preoccupation with the inward personal focus of individual contributor hooks prevent the leader from seeing what is actually happening in the surrounding business environment, it also obscures understanding what information, tools, and support are needed by followers to advance a bigger bet.

The individual contributor hooks are

- taking the credit
- personalizing
- failure to delegate

Invisibility Hooks: These appear as the "Who, Who, Who" hooks. The underlying unknown is, "Will I be viewed fairly?" Invisibility hooks are characterized by the disbelief that everyone is watching. The leader is the barometer of the organization. All its members look to the leader to know how to think and be. To be so visible and critical to the welfare of others can be daunting. Extroverts and introverts both struggle with its consequences. They wrestle with a wide variety of issues, from acting as a cheerleader to being the bearer of bad tidings. Invisibility hooks set in when the leader wants to avoid dealing with the power of office. It is a way of avoiding the reality of being in others' crosshairs, whether life is good or bad.

The twenty-first century has made it harder than ever to protect one's private identity. The premium on transparency now being encoded into organizational policies, the speed of news in the digital age, and the power of the individual arising from social media have made it nearly impossible to control one's image and messaging. That there is a growing industry devoted to online reputation is highly telling.

The desire to protect one's identity as a leader is important. At the same time, being both visible and accessible to followers are critical to connecting with them to go after the leaders' bigger bets. Nevertheless, the urge to avoid that connection is understandable, since with it comes considerable stress.

Invisibility hooks also offer a way of avoiding the inevitable reality that it is lonely at the top. Wandering through that labyrinth in pursuit of bigger bets is a solo activity. While the leaders' job is to take others along, they have to find the drive to lead the way. Stepping back from the reality of connecting with others by hiding in invisibility hooks undermines the ability of a leader to motivate and inspire others.

The invisibility hooks are

- disengagement
- poor boundaries
- inauthenticity

Hooks at a Glance

Hook Categories	Hooks	Description	Underlying Motivators
Operational Hooks		"Do. Do. Do." The task orientation that gets in the way of a broader strategic mindset.	Need for immediate feedback to counter anxiety of not knowing whether a bigger bet will be successful
	Micromanagement	Controlling the work of others with excessive attention to details.	Fear of loss of control
	Perfectionism	Setting a high standard of quality for work that cannot be achieved.	Fear of failure
	Conflict Avoidance	Not engaging in a conflict to avoid the stress of an unknown response from another. Avoidant behaviors include capitulation, disappearance, passive aggression, and bullying.	Fear of standing alone
	Codependence	Making one's own success and happiness dependent on enabling the success and happiness of someone else.	Fear of standing alone
Individual Contributor Hooks		"Me. Me. Me." Thinking in terms of one's own success rather than that of the enterprise.	Concern over one's value to the organization
	Taking the Credit	Taking credit for the accomplishments of others.	Anxiety over importance to the organization
	Personalizing	Not distinguishing one's personal value from the value to the organization.	Lack of self-esteem
	Failure to Delegate	Being unable or reluctant to involve others in the delivery of work.	Lack of trust
Invisibility Hooks		"Who. Who. Who." The disbelief that everyone is watching you.	Resistance to being the barometer of the organization on the basis of which everyone decides what to believe and how to behave
	Disengagement	Withdrawing physically or mentally from involvement in an activity, situation, or personal interaction.	Loss of privacy
	Poor Boundaries	Sharing information with others that is inappropriate for them to receive.	Loss of the validating support of a peer group
	Inauthenticity	Acting in a manner that is inconsistent with one's personality to mask the discomfort of not knowing something.	Fear of being fallible

Going Deeper into Hooks

The hooks within the three thematic buckets each carry with them characteristic behaviors and underlying motivators. Individuals might vary somewhat as to how they exhibit a specific hook, but there are common overall patterns. Similarly, people might have a different motivator from others for adopting a hook. The motivators described here occur with high frequency. What is critical to note is the counterproductive consequences of such hook behaviors. Examples of all ten hooks can be found in the Arrow story and are described in more detail below.

Operational Hooks

Micromanagement: If you do not know what micromanagement is, you have never worked or, for that matter, lived in the world. Micromanagement regrettably appears in many places, and it rarely yields a positive long-term impact.

Underlying micromanaging behavior is a fear of losing control. Rather than waiting for the outcome of moving through the unpredictable twists and turns of the labyrinth, leaders who micromanage direct exactly how each task is to be done. That allows them to see how it turns out right away, rather than coping with the anxiety of waiting to see how it will eventually play out. Instead, they exert their efforts by adjusting fonts, making sure the right people are contacted for a meeting, and reviewing operational history to a microscopic degree to calculate the correct annual expense escalation. All yield results. However, they are not strategic results.

People on the receiving end of micromanagement feel disempowered, apathetic, and end up voting with their feet.

There are times when it is appropriate to be highly directive. When time is of the essence due to an emergency, or a tricky strategic issue arises requiring a high level of expertise, a greater level of direction is appropriate. In situations such as these, a leader needs to stand in front and make the right calls. After the situation has passed, the leader must then step back to allow others to step up.

In the Arrow story, Janelle provides a classic example of micromanagement. Her highly controlling management of the Legal Department established its reputation as the legal dragons, known for their opposition to anything that did not conform to their processes. This is seen in the exchange between Janelle and Arnie about the timing of the IP work he needed for the Porter proposal.

In that conversation, Janelle's need to control both the form and substance of her work ignored the broader strategic issue at stake. Had she focused on the relative importance of what the Porter work could do for Arrow, she might have demonstrated better strategic judgment. Whether Arrow would win the Porter deal was unknown, hence committing to it was uncomfortable for Janelle. However, its large potential upside might well have been worth the risk of moving its IP issue ahead of other assignments in the law department queue.

Perfectionism: Micromanagement involves telling others how to do things. Perfectionism occurs when leaders subject themselves to meeting an impossibly high standard of quality.

Feeding the need for perfectionism is a fear of failure. That fear can also include anxiety about being exposed as a failure or being blamed for it. Fear originates from many sources. It can result from having worked in an unforgiving culture that tolerates no mistakes, growing up in a hypercritical family where failure was never an acceptable option, or enduring a life crisis that elevated a need for feeling safe.

High quality is important. Few would argue against that. However, where it trips the wire of a perfectionist hook is when the high level of quality prevents accomplishment of a bigger bet. The pursuit of perfection can take on a perseverating, grinding quality that creates a closed loop where no output can result. With no output, there can be no accountability. Similarly, since nothing short of perfect scares people hooked by perfectionism, they have to rely on others to tell them when whatever they are doing is ready to go. For these reasons, people caught by perfectionism have a hard time making decisions. Ultimately, it can be a career killer, because executives have to make decisions.

The perfectionist hook caught several Arrow leadership team members. One of them was Claudia, who prided herself in tidy financial reports with no errors. What that meant was that her group provided only the safest of output. While finance is not a place for creative reporting, it also calls for interpretation of data. Even recording how much has been spent on a given line item requires judgment on allocating cost among projects and taking into account the future needs of each. To make that assessment, the leader has to look to the future and decide which way to go, without the benefit of a known outcome.

Conflict Avoidance: Conflict avoidance is one of the top reasons leaders seek executive coaching. Underlying conflict avoidance is a fear of standing alone. In a potential conflict, we do not know how the other person will react to an idea or action. They could agree, disagree, argue, cry, or leave the room. What we know is who we are—what we hold as fundamental values—and what we need from others. Given the uniqueness of who we are and what we want, we enter conflicts alone in our effort to influence others to join us in the pursuit of our bigger bets.

Entering a conflict is not always the best choice of behavior. There are times where the best political maneuver is to stand down from a fight to preserve a needed relationship or cause. When conflict avoidance becomes a hook is where standing down compromises the ability to generate a bigger bet, or simply to do the right thing, something, which in itself, involves risks.

Conflict avoidance shows up in many forms. Below are the four most usually seen:

1. *Capitulation:* Avoiding conflict by going along with others, despite disagreeing with their position.

2. *Disappearance:* Disappearing physically from a situation or mentally leaving it even while physically present.

3. *Passive Aggression:* Remaining silent, saying something non-committal, or signaling displeasure with body language and leaving it to others to figure out what the person really wants.

4. *Bullying:* Taking a strong position and either exiting the scene of potential opposition or counting on others to be intimidated from challenging them to make sure they do not encounter a situation where they might be wrong.

The cost of avoiding conflict is high. Leaders can fail to obtain important information, as was evident throughout the Arrow story when team members did not press one another for answers. It can also lead to receiving mediocre work from others or getting no help at all, leaving leaders to do the work themselves, as was the case for Marco. This not only affects productivity but also has serious career consequences. Instead of focusing on strategies to lift the organization, conflict-avoidance leaders expend their energy on tactical things. The failure to delegate hook has a similar consequence.

A place where conflict avoidance shows up routinely is the failure to give frank and timely feedback to employees. Telling others they either failed to do something or what they did fell below an expected standard definitely can be uncomfortable. You never know if you will be greeted with tears, anger, or debate. You also might learn that you were incorrect in your assessment.

Not entering into the discussion leaves open the consequence that subpar performance is tolerated. It can have a negative impact not only on the underperforming individual, but also has the potential to drag down a whole team. The team could construe the tacit acceptance of an individual's low performance as an indication of the level of quality the leader is willing to accept for the whole group. The team then only works to that lowest common denominator. Lack of feedback can lead to disengagement and retention risk both for the individual and the team.

All the members of the Arrow leadership team demonstrated some kind of conflict avoidance during the story.

Barry capitulated when he stepped away from the abrasive push-back he got from Claudia when he asked for "scrubbed" project reports. Of greater import was his refusal to confront Mark Miller about the way Zinc summarily fired Arrow without explanation. Barry did not trust Mark and saw that as a sufficient reason to avoid meeting with him. However, he had only met him a couple of times and really did not know enough to decide to forego a potentially risky conversation. The cost could have been the Porter deal.

When Barry became angry with Arnie and Marco for the "pissant deals" they had obtained from Claudia, Arnie disappeared from the interaction, watching the tangerine in Barry's hand and saying nothing.

Prickly as he was, Simon serves as an example of passive-aggressive conflict avoidance. With his antisocial exterior, he left others to interpret his displeasure and to work around it, rather than him letting them know what he thought and wanted.

Claudia demonstrates the bullying approach to avoiding conflict. She took hard positions and refused to budge on wider interpretations that she feared she might not understand. Her assumption was that her conflict-avoidant colleagues would not challenge her, which turned out to be correct. They also excluded her whenever possible.

Codependence: This hook is a first cousin of conflict avoidance. It also stems from not wanting to stand alone and appears behaviorally as conflict avoidance. The concept, born in the addiction research, appears in business as making one's own happiness dependent on the happiness of others. It can be seen where the leader will avoid calling out someone on an action that is not the best business choice in order to pre-serve the relationship the leader has with that person. This often occurs between former coworkers whose shared history includes accommodations made for each other in the past that engender credit in the present.

Michael, Janey's marketing associate, represents a classic exam-ple of codependence. His main goal at work was to make sure she was happy. It meant that he did nothing that might disrupt her direction. It also holds him back in his career. Said however facetiously, Barry was willing to fire him for cleaning out all the licorice jellybeans. If Michael had exhibited any independent thought, Barry might have felt more charitably toward him.

The meeting between Barry and Nigel on crafting a customer service description for Porter reinforced a codependence between them. Coming up with something safe gave them a comfortable, enjoyable conversation rather than the messy talk that would have likely taken place if they both set to decon-structing the Zinc puzzle.

Individual Contributor Hooks

Taking the Credit: This hook goes to the question of "Am I important?" In order to align the efforts of others, leaders need to recognize that people want recognition for the value they cre-ate for an organization. Many human resource studies through-out the years have concluded that while compensation is not inconsequential in a decision to leave an organization, a more important reason for leaving a company is employee belief that they were not appreciated for their work.

Few behaviors ruin the motivation of workers more than when credit for their work is taken by someone else. It leads to reduced performance and increased retention risk. Janey accused Barry of stealing the credit for bringing in Porter as a potential client. Regardless of whether that was actually true, her perception of Barry demotivated her. It caused her to distrust him and become unwilling to do her best work. Instead, she spent her time roaming the halls complaining about him to Nigel and Arnie.

Personalizing: This hook arises from a difficulty with distinguishing between "What is my value to the organization?" and "What is my value as a human being?" The former is where leaders need to focus. The latter speaks of fractured self-esteem. When someone is told, often in fierce and unflattering words, "That presentation was awful!" a leader who is hooked by personalizing would hear that feedback as "You are awful!"

While it is possible that there might be a personal issue between the individuals in the conversation, most of the time, there is not. People are too concerned with delivery of something and their own success to worry about the worth of the other person, sad as that might be. Therefore, the negativity usually emanates from a variety of circumstances related to the presentation that has nothing to do with the leader and might or might not have been within that person's control.

Personalizing is a common hook. It is difficult when things go wrong in an organization not to experience failure as personal. After all, you are the person who tried to make something work. However, to see a failure as a judgment of your worth as a human being is a slippery slope that is the wrong way to go and will not guide you to an effective solution.

The Arrow story contains numerous examples of personalizing. Barry saw the Porter question about why Zinc fired the company as a personal affront. Instead of looking for factors external to him about why Porter might be interested in the Zinc termination, he instead felt devalued, believing he did "everything to earn their trust . . . And this is my reward?" Confusing his personal value with the broader situation prevented Barry from understanding the motivation behind Porter's question about Zinc that was of benefit to Arrow.

Janey could only see Barry's distraction from the Porter response as a comment on her self-worth, when instead Barry was consumed with avoiding his feelings of failure about losing the Zinc project.

Failure to Delegate: Failure to delegate can be caused merely by lack of experience assigning work to other people. That is a skills issue. More typically, and where it becomes a hook, is when it involves a lack of trust in how others will perform.

Giving away control over work requires courage. What is not known is how the delegated activity will turn out. The delegated work could be of lower quality than if the leader had done it. Leaders might fear it would reflect badly on them. Conversely, it might produce a better product. This could cause problems for a leader who fears losing power or status if someone else does a better job. In either case, the real cost is failure of the leader to build a strong team that will deepen the talent pool of the organization and strengthen the leader's ability to take it to new horizons.

Marco hated dealing with customer complaints. He loathed even more asking his staff to take on the pressure of managing those complaints. If they did not handle it right, his problems would get worse. In crisis situations, the leader has to decide whether he or she has enough time to train the team how to manage its issues. Ideally, the leader has trained the team ahead of time. However, too often, the leader has not allocated adequate training time.

With or without training, the reluctance of a leader to trust others to do the work can cause the leader to decide not to delegate at all. The consequence is that the team does not grow, and the leader works overtime on tactical rather than strategic activities. Marco yearned to build more innovative project management systems, but never could seem to find the time to do that. Had he been willing to delegate more of his daily work to his team, he might have found the time. It is worth noting that to do that, he also would have had to face the frightening prospect of not knowing how his innovations would be received, which might be one of the reasons he was hooked.

Invisibility Hooks

Disengagement: This hook appears as a reaction to loss of privacy. When people become leaders, they lose the ability to manage successfully how they are viewed. As barometers of their organizations, they can count on being in somebody's field of vision at any time, in person or online.

Living with this public persona can be trying and difficult to sustain. Leaders take on the risks to achieve great things, and their rewards can often be a hail of criticism. A common reaction to this state of affairs is to disengage from the reality of the situation, in the moment or on a more prolonged basis. Both have the impact of breaking the connection needed to motivate and inspire those who work with them.

Disengagement can occur in a physical way, literally withdrawing from a physical setting. It also can happen mentally. Leaders might be in the room physically, but their minds can be somewhere else, a place that feels less challenging and scary.

Barry in the Arrow story disengaged on numerous occasions. His tendency to hide in the Excelsior project occurred when he did not know what was going on or what to do. Rather than endure the stress of delving into the truth, he disappeared into his Excelsior spreadsheet. This tendency first appears at the beginning of the story. To avoid the anxiety from thinking about his contribution to the negative results he saw in the financial report, he went straight to the Excelsior file.

Simon felt unappreciated for his work saving the company from the Trash debacle. Feeling unappreciated often sets the disengagement hook in motion. Instead of engaging in a conversation with Barry on his status in the company, he retreated into dark matter and other diversions. His disengagement prevented him from digging into the Zinc mystery until late in the day (literally). Had he not finally discovered a core driver of loving his reputation as the Lion King of Coders, his refusal to release his disengagement hook could have had major repercussions for the Porter deal and for Arrow's future.

Poor Boundaries: Leadership is lonely. There are many feelings and thoughts you cannot share with others. When people become leaders, they lose the former peers with whom they had vetted ideas and gained support. Once someone is promoted above the level of his or her peers, that informal but vital sounding board disappears. The leader then finds himself or herself wandering in those unknown corridors without the comfort of known peers with whom the leader could test ideas and be validated.

For example, a leader might become responsible for the compensation decisions for former peers requiring knowledge of new policies and information that cannot be shared with them. However inappropriate, leaders often make unflattering, off-the-cuff remarks to a former peer about a person with whom they had worked together as peers. Denigration of someone in that circumstance can lead to both negative cultural and legal consequences.

Barry complained to Arnie about Janelle, Simon, and Claudia. It did not advance Arnie's ability to gather information from those persons and sent a message that they could be disrespected, regardless of Barry's true opinion of them.

Inauthenticity: Effective leadership depends on credibility. For followers to trust a leader, the leader must be a person with whom they can connect, someone who comes across as real and authentic. When leaders are inauthentic, they lose their power to influence. An underlying reason is a fear of being fallible.

Leaders often mistakenly believe they have to know all the answers to questions or concerns. However, if they are truly fulfilling their role as leaders, surveying the far horizons for clues leading to bigger bets, they cannot possibly know everything. What a leader does have to know is how to pursue answers and to ask for help when doing so.

Nigel put on his game face with Barry to discuss the Porter questions. Underneath he felt weary and preoccupied with his problems at home. His disconnected, glib banter with Barry on how Arrow treated its customers and how he could write that up for Porter did little to resolve the underlying issue of the real reason for Zinc's termination or to advance the Arrow proposal.

Overcoming Hooks to Achieve Bigger Bets: Building a New Hook Cycle

The Old Hook Cycle: Overcoming hooks and their negative impacts on achieving bigger bets starts with recognizing when they appear. Hooks surface in many ways and vary by the individual. As shown in Diagram A, a hook grabs hold in response to a triggering event that causes discomfort.

DIAGRAM A
Old and New Hook Cycles

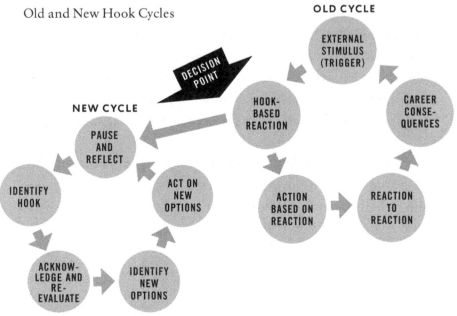

Here are some examples:

- Your client gives you a tough assignment with an unforgiving schedule.

- A team member angrily confronts you during a group meeting about project results.

- The leader of another group steals your idea and takes credit for it.

- A core company strategy is failing to work with a key customer.

The trigger sets off a chain reaction that if not stopped could lead to negative results for you, the organization, and your bigger bets.

Consider the following scenario, using Claudia from the Arrow story as an example:

As the story opens, we see Claudia slide into Barry's office to sniff out what Arnie ran in to tell Barry. She behaves in a coy, disingenuous manner. Rather than folding her into the conversation, Barry shuts her out, giving Claudia no choice but to leave. Later in the story Barry visits Claudia to obtain better project margin reports for Porter. There we have clues as to why Barry did not earlier include Claudia in the conversation with Arnie.

Acting on her perfectionist hook, Claudia refused to give Barry any report she did not think was perfect, with each component triple-checked and confirmed for accuracy. Barry responded angrily, departing from Claudia's office thinking how obstructive she was and wanting to distance himself from her. Because of her unbending, narrow-minded behavior, Barry did not include Claudia in broader strategic discussions. As far as he was concerned, Claudia would not progress as an important contributor to the executive team. He saw her value limited to pristine financial reports and her relationship with the chair of the board.

This is Claudia's old hook cycle. Hearing from Barry that he needed something more responsive to the Porter request than a polished, completely vetted, business-as-usual report triggered her. To satisfy his request, Claudia had to stretch beyond her comfort zone, which scared her. It would have been better had she looked at what would best satisfy Porter and how she could accommodate that request. Instead, because paying attention to the requests of potential customers was not in her repertoire of known constituents, not to mention known responses, she refused to honor Barry's request.

Her trigger appeared in the form of anger and catalyzed her perfectionist hook. She knew this reaction well from a life history of highly critical, judgmental parents. In the moment at work, she reacted in a familiar pattern of lashing out at the person she experienced as the attacker, namely Barry. Defaulting to a rigid high standard put Claudia in familiar territory.

The perfectionist behavior gave her a false sense of safety with her parents, supposedly protecting her from their criticism. It did not work, as was later seen, when they did not even acknowledge her winning the finance industry award. Unfortunately, she had transferred her perfectionism to the work setting, where such behavior was counterproductive. Her obsession with holding to a sharp, perfectionist standard distanced her from Barry and the rest of the leadership team. As a consequence, she failed to advance the Porter bigger bet or her own career goal of being part of the leadership team strategy discussions.

The New Cycle: To rectify this situation, Claudia had to build a new cycle that would push past her perfectionist hook to find a way to support the Porter bigger bet and, ultimately, her career. The pivot point lay at the beginning, where Claudia needed to recognize that she had been hooked. Hooks can be experienced in many different ways and vary by the individual. Some people notice strong anxiety, annoyance, or even dead calm as they distance themselves from the stress caused by the situation. In Claudia's case, her hook appeared in the form of extreme anger that caused her to attack others.

When Claudia became aware she had been hooked, she had a decision to make. She could let old habits assert themselves and go into an attack mode. Alternatively, she could form a new and more effective strategy. That starts the creation of a new cycle.

As shown in Diagram B, the steps of creating a new cycle are as follows:

Recognize Triggering External Stimulus: The new cycle begins with the awareness that a hook has grabbed hold. You might not know at the time what hook it is. However, to start a new pattern of behavior, it is enough to recognize you have been triggered by something and are responding defensively with a hook.

Pause and Reflect: Taking a deep breath, becoming quiet, doing anything that breaks the pathos of the hook reaction will start the switch to a new cycle. It stops the speeding train of defensive behavior. It also sets in motion a mode of detachment from the stress of the situation. Detachment enables people to open their field of vision, much like an aperture on a camera, to see more broadly what is "going on in the room."

It lets you see factors influencing the situation that you could not see before due to focus on what was happening to you, rather than in the room. When the aperture starts to open, you can perceive what you did not know before—who is engaged, who has the best information, who has objections, who is confused, and who is driving the conversation. With the benefit of more information, you can form a new and more successful response.

Identify the Hook: Identifying what hook is active for you will help you understand its characteristics and map a new strategy. Claudia realized that she reacted to Barry's action as an attack on her carefully processed, mistake-proof financial reporting. With that observation, she could identify a perfectionist hook.

Acknowledge and Re-evaluate: When a hook takes hold, it is easy to beat yourself up for less-than-ideal behavior. However, it is useful to remember that hooks serve as defenses to mitigate the pain caused by something. There is nothing wrong with that. Where it becomes a problem is if your reaction creates a barrier to moving toward a bigger bet. To recognize and modify your behavior to unhook the hook, it helps first to give yourself compassion. We are all flawed humans trying to make our way in life. Cutting ourselves some emotional slack while we work on learning new things will facilitate the process of change.

After her conversation with Janelle, Claudia began to work through her shame about being obstructionist with Barry when he requested different reports. It allowed her to step back to see the negative consequences of her behavior—she was not advancing the Porter proposal or the quality of her career. Then, she could proceed in a less emotionally charged manner to choose reports that would advance the Porter proposal and satisfy Barry.

Identify New Options: Once the emotional clutter is removed through detachment, acknowledgment, and looking more broadly at a situation, you can identify new and more effective strategies to handle a situation.

Act on New Options: When Claudia applied her new options, that is, the broader purpose of winning valuable new client work and advancing her career, she delivered to the Arrow leadership team the reports that supported smart project management. She also went on to expand her contribution to the company by shadowing members of the Operations and Engineering teams

DIAGRAM B
Claudia's Old and New Hook Cycles

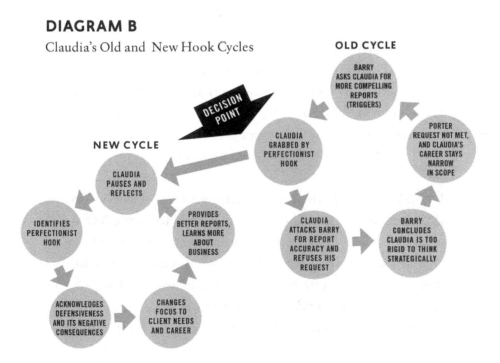

to learn more about the business. She increased likelihood of a stronger connection to the team by becoming willing to share her more vulnerable, human side. Bringing her daughter to work and showing her pride in her daughter was a major step for her.

How Do You Break Out of Your Hooks Longer Term?

On-Stage Work: Hooks tend to show up by surprise, appearing when you are least prepared. A new customer calls out of the blue to tell you how badly they think your project with them is going. You learn from a peer that a project you championed was pilloried in the press. A team member attacks you at a meeting in front of your direct reports. There is no doubt these are difficult moments. They are also opportunities.

Learning to recognize your hooks in the moment and finding a more successful strategy is the "on-stage" work. On-stage work involves learning to become aware that a hook has caught you at the moment it occurs. Then you use your awareness to stop a reactive "hooked" mode, regroup in the moment, and adopt a better strategy for you and the organization.

Off-Stage Work: To sustain learning to recognize hooks and strategies to overcome them, it is important to do the "off-stage" work. Off-stage work centers on understanding what set off your hook in the first place. We all travel with personal history that encodes into our behavior, often below our level of consciousness. Its influence can be profound both on our feelings and actions. Discovering the source of our hooks empowers us to make better choices.

There are many ways to unearth the roots of our feelings. Paying attention to our feelings is an obvious beginning. From there, we can learn more by a wide range of tools including journaling, insight from colleagues and friends, reading relevant literature, coaching, and therapy.

In her conversation with Janelle on the impact of family history, Claudia started her own inner reflection. Her reflection was further reinforced by her son's observations of her contradictory behavior at work. The daughter of emotionally distant parents, she grew up in an environment where she rarely received their attention. Instead of her parents reinforcing her value as a human being, they ignored or criticized her efforts, no matter how hard she tried. As a child, she did not know any better than to internalize the judgment that she was unworthy of attention.

With the help of collegial support and the love of her children, she began to separate her sense of self-worth from the issues of her parents. While the instinct remained to default to a perfectionist hook when things went wrong at work, she learned through awareness and practice to separate what was going on in her company from reliving the negative lessons learned from her parents.

4. Drivers

Drivers are the highly individualized purposes that propel you into the future, feeding your appetite to build something and to lead people there, no matter what it takes. To navigate through the discomfort caused by the unknown, leaders need a goal or broader purpose to motivate them to push forward.

Drivers provide purpose, an endpoint that makes the stress of getting past their hooks worthwhile. They generate fuel for leaders to travel through the scary places of the labyrinth as they go after bigger bets.

Drivers vary with the bigger bets and with the people pursuing them. They can be practical and relevant to one particular situation. These are called situational drivers. They also can come from a deeper place based on deep personal values, life stories, and dreams for the future. These are called core drivers.

Situational drivers relate to a specific situation. For example, a law firm partner wants to prove to his partners that he is a "player" when it comes to business development. To be a player, he has to make public speeches in front of industry groups and other potential clients. Giving speeches terrifies him. However, the disdain he feels from his partners about his inability to attract new business is so galling that the partner takes the scary step of joining Toastmasters International to learn how to give speeches more confidently.

In 2011, the Japanese women's soccer team won the Women's World Cup, to the astonishment of many. In Japan, only about 25,000 women played soccer at the time. It was a major accomplishment for them to participate in the Women's World Cup. Yet they did and won. When interviewed after the tournament about what motivated them in this amazing achievement, the team members said that they wanted to restore the honor of Japan. They felt shame for their country because of the 2011 tsunami and consequent meltdown of the Fukushima Daiichi nuclear power plant reactors.

One could argue with them that they had no reason to feel shame. After all, they certainly did not cause the tsunami. However, that argument was irrelevant to them. Equating winning with restoring honor to the country, regardless of whether the country actually had suffered dishonor, served as a strong situational driver for the soccer team. As history showed, it worked.

Core drivers provide a deeper, more fundamental kind of fuel. They are an "I have a dream" kind of motivator. Core drivers emerge from life experiences that create a deeply molding impact on the leader. They can come from positive experiences— a supportive high school coach, the sage advice of a special teacher, the feeling of a team that pulled into a unified group that wins a championship, or a reinforcing relative who shared important wisdom.

Virgin Group's Sir Richard Branson cites his influential ninety-nine-year-old grandmother as a deep personal motivator. She said to him, "You've got one go in life, so make the most of it."

More often core drivers arise from early life and result from frightening or difficult events.

Nelson Mandela and His Rugby World Cup Bigger Bet: One example of a core driver that emerged from hard times is the story of revolutionary politician Nelson Mandela and his pursuit of the Rugby World Cup, when he was the first black president of South Africa. Nelson Mandela endured the extreme difficulty of apartheid, including twenty-seven years in a small prison cell for his activities related to fighting for racial equality. When he was released and became the president of South Africa, he spearheaded many enormous bigger bets.

One bigger bet was portrayed in the Clint Eastwood 2009 film, *Invictus*. The film describes the early days of Mandela's presidency. Mandela held the strong belief that he would not be a victim. After so many years of his adult life in prison, he could easily have seen himself as a supreme victim. Instead, he used his time in prison to study his jailers and learn more about the white South African society.

He concluded that for South Africa to succeed as a nation where the white people constituted only 10 percent of the population but nevertheless controlled the economy, courts, and police, black and colored people would have to unite with the whites. The film depicts the many risky and tenacious maneuvers Mandela made in pursuit of his bigger bet to align all South Africans, regardless of race, around winning the 1995 Rugby World Cup.

As was witnessed by the world, South Africa won the Rugby World Cup with the support of black, white, and colored South Africans. Mandela achieved his bigger bet. An important source of strength and motivation through many risky and scary situations was his strong core driver that he would not be a victim. Following the English poet William E. Henley's 1875 poem "Invictus," which he kept in his jail cell, Mandela drew inspiration from the final two lines, "I am the master of my fate; I am the captain of my soul."

The Story of a Young Executive: A few years ago at a conference in Canada on the Journey of Not Knowing, I asked the audience of women executives to share with one another their stories about a challenge they had in their life and what got them through it that they later applied to their professional lives.

The 160 executives in the room quickly leapt into conversations. The room grew louder with enthusiastic talking. After several minutes we reconvened. I asked the audience members whether anyone wanted to tell her story to the whole group. This led to a lot of mumbling and nervous looks around the room. Finally, a hand popped up and a woman said, "I have to share the story I heard from this woman next to me." I asked the woman next to her if she was okay with that or would she rather speak for herself. Not surprisingly, she chose the latter.

Her mother worked as a cleaner in a large office building. Because the building was full of office workers during the day, she had to work at night. When this woman was young, she usually stayed at home with her father or another relative while her mother worked. One night when she was five years old, she accompanied her mother to the office building, because there was no childcare available at home.

Late in the evening, she and her mother entered the office of the company CEO. As her mother started to clean, the girl looked around and spied a big, heavily upholstered desk chair. Being five years old, she did what any self-respecting five year old would do. She ran and jumped into that big chair and swiveled back and forth in it several times.

When her mother saw this, she shouted at her daughter in horror, "You get out of that chair!"

"Why?" asked the puzzled five year old.

"You don't belong there. You will NEVER sit in that chair!"

The woman at the conference could still remember how she felt that night. She was astonished, then angry at what her mother said. She vividly recalled saying to herself, "Oh, yes, I will!"

When she told us her story at the conference, we learned that she was the CEO of her own property management company with twenty-five employees. Many things got her there, but an important force that propelled her to take the risky path toward achieving her goal was the core driver her mother's words had created in her.

In the Arrow story, each leadership team member found a driver to propel him or her through the discomfort of the unknown. Some chose situational drivers.

Nigel wanted to honor his wife's support of his need to take care of his mother and sister by taking home to her the Porter bonus on which she had been counting. When Janelle cracked open the door by confessing to him in front of the whole team that she "did not know" anything about his life, a foundation might have been laid for him to delve deeper for a core driver later on.

Other members of the team went deeper to discover core drivers.

Marco wanted to prove to his father that he could make it in the technology business.

Claudia came to the realization that her perfectionist behavior at work did not produce anything that won the admiration she craved from her detached parents or allowed her to develop her strategic abilities. Worse, it caused her to act in an adversarial, difficult way that alienated her colleagues, people she actually valued. What finally started her journey to unhook from her perfectionism was the core driver to inspire her beloved children to know it was okay to make mistakes and be human.

Barry recognized how his perfectionist fear of failure had caused him to disengage from the messiness of facing the unknown reasons for losing the Zinc deal and also the Porter opportunity. Barry did not want to repeat the life of his father, a perfectionist, unhappy man who did not connect with anything but his clean car and golf clubs. Instead, Barry shook loose of his disengagement and perfectionism. He wanted to connect to what was really happening in his own life and with his team. The core driver of connecting galvanized him to solve the Zinc mystery and win the Porter bigger bet.

It is unlikely that any of these persons will discard their hooks completely. We all revert to old tendencies, particularly in times of high stress. However, our commitment to noticing when a hook is catching us, switching to a different strategy, and calling on a meaningful driver to chase after a bigger bet will decrease the power of the hook and point us forward.

We cannot change our life stories,
but we can change how we behave as a result of them.

Adding Drivers to Fuel the New Cycle

Overcoming hooks first by recognizing them, then adopting new strategies will go far toward improving the outcome. What will improve the sustainability of the journey is to add a driver to the equation, as shown in Diagram C. The driver provides motivation for reworking one's approach and managing the discomfort of facing unknown results.

DIAGRAM C
New Hook Cycle with a Driver

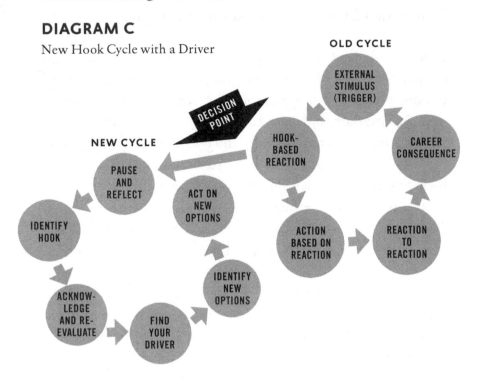

The Impact of Experience on Navigating the Unknown

Experience will help with the discomfort of not knowing as you practice working though ambiguity, unhooking hooks, and surfacing drivers. However, if you are delivering on your role as a leader, anticipating the newest needs of your customers, you will never find a place of complete comfort. Comfort sits in the middle of what is known, and people are already doing that.

Part 5

THE REWARD OF TAKING THE JOURNEY:
ONE NIGHT AT AMAZON IN LATE
DECEMBER 1999

Finding My Core Driver

I LIVED THE first half of my childhood in Colorado Springs, Colorado. Surrounding me was a pristine environment of topaz skies and rarefied Rocky Mountain air. We lived next to Colorado College, a warm, vibrant academic community. Rising each morning with the strong outline of 14,110-foot Pikes Peak presiding over the landscape and the congenial college nearby created a deep awe in me of the power of environments, physical and human. That appreciation traveled with me into my adult life, taking form in my interest in urban development and the dynamics of organizational growth.

Later in life when I reflected on what drove me as a leader, I thought back on those Colorado origins. They definitely influenced my choices. However, what really propelled me was something deeper and far more personal.

I grew up in the 1950s and 1960s when girls were expected to be pretty, supportive, and relatively well-behaved. Our future was to be an arm ornament for a handsome Ken-doll type or the handsome actor-musician Ricky Nelson, whoever showed up first. As far as I was concerned, the being pretty part was a nonstarter for me, because I had red hair and freckles. In that era, no fashion models in magazines ever had red hair and definitely not freckles. Clearly I did not qualify as a future arm ornament. I also was not particularly well-behaved. Coming from a family of five children, rough-and-tumble play reigned supreme. For the same reason, "supportive" went out the window, at least in any way that was too obvious, although without question it would come through on important things.

I watched my mother and her friends work hard at running their houses, play ferocious bridge, and smile diplomatically at their husband's jokes, whether or not they were funny. I thought those women were plenty smart and capable. What I did not understand was why so many seemed to be treated in such a patronizing, second-class citizen way. Few of those women seemed to be having a good time. They smoked their cigarettes and often looked tired. It was the era of the pre-feminist Mad Men, and what I saw were Mad Women.

Looking back many years with the benefit of an adult perspective, I have no idea what really went on between husbands and wives or with their friends. However, what created a driver for me was hatched from what I perceived as a child. When I thought about the core driver that provided the most fuel during my years as a leader, I finally realized that what drove me was the strong desire to "count." I wanted to be treated with the same respect as those men back in my childhood. I did not need to be better than anyone. What I wanted were the same opportunities as others to enter as an equal into the places where things were happening.

Needing to count gave me the fuel to pursue many different adventures, often in entrepreneurial settings, either as a lawyer, executive, or executive advisor. In my executive role at Amazon, needing to count carried me through many trying times.

To succeed at Amazon, leaders had to generate constant bigger bets. It made it fun, fascinating, and exhausting. In its early days, there were a few particularly large bigger bets that informed our work. "Work hard, have fun, and make history." "Be the most customer-centric company in the world." "Get big fast." These were the three biggest slogans during my time at the company.

In 1999, Wall Street still doubted that Amazon had a viable business model. For all of us proud overachievers and especially the many people with MBA degrees who resided in our leader ranks, this was particularly infuriating. While adopting a view toward the long-term, per the vision of our CEO, we also had more near-term goals.

I don't recall it being officially published within the company, but those of us running the Operations and Real Estate departments knew that to prove to the world that Amazon had a viable business model, 99 percent of the Christmas orders had to hit the door of their intended destinations by the close of business on December 23, 1999.

For that to happen, the website, front and back, had to work; all the real estate had to be in place; the twenty-first-century fulfillment system had to be designed, programmed, and installed; and the supply chain had to be working to procure, process, and send goods to the millions upon millions of waiting customers all over the globe.

In my world of real estate and corporate services, that year we acquired and built almost five million square feet of real estate and supporting infrastructure worldwide. All this had to be done in the eight months between January and August. We moved at a hyper speed, eliminated any and all excess processes, and went right to the heart of what had to be done. Designs that normally required weeks and twenty pages of blueprints were drawn in the aisles of airplanes and reduced to six pages. Even with radical procedures, buildings got built without codes being bypassed, permits missed, or, amazingly, budgets exceeded.

Motivating the team was both easy and challenging. We all wanted to win, to prove to the world that we had something worthwhile, and doing that was new and hard.

Early in the evening of December 23, 1999, I sat alone in my office, exhausted but peaceful. I had just worked my last shift in the local fulfillment center. Most of the office staff had gone home and, for a brief moment, there was nothing else to do.

At approximately six thirty p.m., the email landed in my inbox, *"As of the end of business today, 99 percent of our packages arrived at the doors of their customers."* I stared at the message in disbelief. We had delivered! Somehow throughout that long, harrowing year, I never thought we would fail. I also hadn't really fathomed how it would feel to succeed.

For no reason that I can remember, I rose from my desk and walked in a daze into the hall and crossed the lobby over to the Operations Department. At the same time, coming slowly from that wing were five leaders from Operations, including its new senior vice president, Finance director, Supply Chain vice president, and Operations analyst. At first, none of us said anything. We all arrived simultaneously at one random spot in the hall and stood silently in a small circle for a few seconds looking at one another. Then, as if on cue, we gasped together, "We did it!!!!"

It was an electric moment—one I will never forget. We were so proud and grateful for all that had been achieved.

It had been a long, twisty journey through the labyrinth for me and the team members who traveled by my side. They did not hear me mumble to myself in the darkest, scariest moments, "I want to count." Instead, they heard me coach, fret, carp, and congratulate. They all had their own reasons to follow, and to lead in their own areas. In the end, when we poked our heads out of that labyrinth, we knew we had done something fantastic.

Leadership is not like any other job. It is a challenge, honor, and opportunity to make a difference. Entering the unknown releases its possibilities and allows us to lead others to make the future happen. Being comfortable with the discomfort of not knowing is not easy. It calls on us to find our inner compass, see the world without varnish, and trust that no matter how scary it gets, if we keep navigating those twisted pathways toward building something better, we will arrive there.

Appendix
Arrow Leadership Team Members Hooks and Drivers

Arrow Leadership Team Member	Title Department	Hooks	Driver
Barry	Chief Executive Officer, Founder	Disengagement, conflict avoidance (capitulating), poor boundaries, taking the credit (Janey's perception that Barry needed to correct), perfectionism, codependence	Not be like his perfectionist, disconnected father (core).
Claudia	Chief Financial Officer	Inauthenticity, perfectionism, conflict avoidance (bully, passive aggressive), personalizing	Be an inspiration for her children to feel free to make mistakes and be human (core).
Janelle	General Counsel Legal	Perfectionism, conflict avoidance (bully), micromanagement	Make order out of the chaos for the people who are important to her (core)
Simon	Vice President Engineering	Disengagement, conflict avoidance (passive aggressive)	Be seen as extremely smart, the Lion King of Coders (core).
Nigel	Vice President Sales	Inauthenticity, conflict avoidance (bully), disengagement, codependence	To honor his wife's support of his need to take care of his mother and sister by taking home to her the Porter bonus (situational).
Marco	Vice President Operations	Conflict avoidance (capitulation), failure to delegate, codependence	Prove to his father that he could succeed in the tech world, and keep his values (core), and (situational) get Anthony to make up for getting him fired.
Arnie	Assistant Vice President Sales	Conflict avoidance (disappearance/ capitulation)	Get out from under the humiliation caused by bullies (core).
Janey	Director Marketing	Personalizing, conflict avoidance (bully); her assistant, Michael, is codependent	Wanting to be well regarded by her mother (core).

Acknowledgments

If I have learned nothing else during the past two years, it is that writing a book draws from a lifetime of experiences. Even more so, it relies upon a lifetime of support from family, colleagues, and friends. There are not enough pages in the world to thank everyone who inspired the writing and production of this book. However, I will attempt to name the ones closest to this process, with apologies for failure to mention others specifically.

I want to start by thanking my daughter and husband, who have listened to me churn through endless ideas on how or even whether to write a book. Additional recognition goes to my husband, who once I crossed the threshold into book writing, read countless drafts, searched for synonyms, clarified awkward turns of phrases, and reminded me that what I was doing was worthy.

Invaluable support also came from my sisters and their families, who know what it is to strive, get nervous, and still keep going. They lived with me through the journey of not knowing in life, far beyond this book.

Next but certainly not lower on the list of persons to thank is my business partner in The Journey of Not Knowing, LLC, Stephanie Reynolds. She believed in the core premise of the Journey of Not Knowing and went on to co-create with me a full leadership development program around it. I also want to acknowledge the rest of the Journey team members who have delivered programs, written copy, made improving suggestions, and assembled endless packages of materials.

Critically important thanks goes to Gail Kearns, my indispensable and fabulous book Sherpa, who with her To Press & Beyond team, provided the smart, insightful, and essential adult supervision I needed to take this book from early draft to a fully edited, produced, and distributed book. Without that help, no one would be reading this page.

I also want to thank *the*BookDesigners, whose ability to translate the book contents into an imaginative, accurate book cover and interior design made a compelling difference. For the design of the Journey website, my thanks go to Heidi Hackler of Dolphin Design Studio for her beautiful and innovative work along with Eric Amundson of IvyCat who provided the development support.

I am grateful and give thanks to Ilene Segalove, who in addition to providing cogent editorial and artistic feedback at critical times, kept me focused on my own creative edge. She also reminded me that it was okay to be vulnerable and honor my own life story.

Deep thanks go to Susan Cannon, Asuka Nakahara, Gail Ayers, Patricia Langer, and Cindy Aden, who did me the supreme honor of reading the manuscript and providing their endorsements of the work. I also want to recognize my early readers, my husband, Katherine Koberg, Harriet Cannon, Marilyn Hawkins, Brenda Bluemke, and Gail Resnik, who slaved through first and second drafts to help convert a plausible story with a lot of moving parts into a book with an integrated message.

For the opportunity to teach and work with a dynamic cross section of executives from around the world, I want to thank Gene Kohn of Kohn Pedersen Fox, who asked me to help him launch and subsequently lead the "Challenges of Leadership" program for executives at Harvard Graduate School of Design. I want to give a special thank you to Corlette Moore McCoy, Former Founder & Executive Director of the Office of Executive Education for the Harvard Graduate School of Design, with whom I had a wonderful ten-year partnership co-developing the Challenges of Leadership Program. The work we did together also contributed to the inspiration for the Journey of Not Knowing program. I'd also like to thank the GSD OEE staff who made the program happen.

A group of people whose names could fill volumes would be my tenacious, fun, and hardworking team at Amazon and our many contractors and consultants. Without all those persons, there would have been no way we could have worked hard, had fun, and made history together.

Finally, out of respect for their privacy, I will not name but want to thank my many valued clients from fifteen years of coaching work who have trusted me with their stories, worked hard to become stronger as leaders, and shared insights into leadership life beyond my own. I also want to assure all of them that none of them appears in the Arrow story.

Discussion Questions

The following are questions to ask yourself or discuss in a group about your relationship with the unknown, pursuing new possibilities, and getting past your resistance to change.

PART 1
What Amazon Taught Me About
Leadership and the Unknown

1. *"...company strategy traveled at the speed of bits and bytes and real estate travels at the speed of bricks." (Page 2)*

   • Have you ever found yourself out of sync with the environment around you? How did it feel?

2. *"Not knowing was scary, and scary was okay." (Page 3)*

   • How are you with "scary"? What does the word evoke for you?

3. *"I am here to learn." (Page 27)*

   • When you find yourself in a situation where you don't understand what is going on, how do you normally respond? Does that response work for you? If not, what might work better?

4. *"Where there is high speed, high stakes, and high ambiguity, anxiety rules the day." (page 31)*

   • What is your experience with rapid change and how do you deal (or not deal) with it? What have you learned from your experience that has helped you to manage rapid change?

5. *"As a leader, you have to know who you are and for what you stand. You have to know your values, personal history, and dreams for the future." (Page 36)*

   • What navigation lights guide you as a leader or in your personal life? In times of stress, what shows you the way?

PART 2
Leadership and the Unknown

6. *"The primary function of a leader is to pursue new strategic ideas or 'bigger bets.'" (Page 49)*

   • Think of someone you know either at work or in your personal life who is good at creating bigger bets. What do you notice about the person you admire? What can you learn from that person?

7. *". . . successful leaders push forward" (Page 50)*

   • What happens to you after experiencing a difficult situation? Do you move on, obsess, check out, analyze it for lessons, discuss it with a friend or colleague . . . ?

8. *"The road to success is paved with failures." (Page 51)*

   • What is your relationship with failure? Think of a time when something you did failed. How did you respond to it? Looking back at that time now, what did you learn that you carry into your current life?

9. *"We have to deal with the world the way it is, not as we would like it to be." (Page 58)*

   • How accurately do you believe you see situations? What

makes you believe that? What would others say about how accurately you perceive situations? What affects how you see and remember experiences, particularly difficult ones?

PART 3
Arrow, Inc.: One Day in March

10. At the beginning of the story, how would you describe the Arrow team? If you had been hired as an executive coach for the team at the beginning of the story, what would have been your initial assessment? How would you describe the team at the end of the story?

11. As you followed the characters around the halls of Arrow, did their conversations or actions evoke anything in your current work environment or personal life? Did you find yourself cringing at any point? When and why?

12. Is there any resemblance between the Arrow team and your team or group? If so, what?

13. Did any of Arrow characters seem familiar to you? Who and why? Did you see yourself in any of those characters?

14. What are some examples of hooks that appeared in the story? What hooks do you see yourself using?

15. What did you learn from some of the main characters' background stories that helped you understand what motivated them and what held them back?

16. What are some examples of drivers the main characters used to push past their reluctance to deal with the Zinc firing?

PART 4
The Journey of Not Knowing Model

Bigger bets:

> *"Strategic new ideas that lie in the unknown and propel you to create a stronger, more successful organization."*

- What dreams do you have to make something better for your organization, team, community, or personal life?

The risks of the unknown.

> *"The risks you encounter when you move into the unfamiliar world of the unknown to pursue bigger bets."*

- Think of an idea you have wanted to try out but felt uncomfortable pursuing. What thoughts and feelings get in your way?

Hooks

> *"Defensive behaviors that give you short-term relief from the discomfort of the risks of the unknown, but will prevent you from reaching your bigger bets."*

- What defensive behaviors do you tend to use? How well do they work for you?

- Look at the chart on page 215 and the descriptions of hooks on pages 211 to 214. Do you recognize any of the hooks? Which ones? Think of an experience when you behaved defensively and were "hooked." What started it, and how did it end?

Drivers

"Your personal motivators that provide fuel to move you through the discomfort from the risks of the unknown toward achieving bigger bets."

- Think of a difficult time you experienced and overcame at work or in your personal life. What driver helped you to get through it?

If you enjoyed this book, please consider posting a review on your blog, Amazon, Goodreads, and/or Barnes & Noble. If you send a link to your review to julie@juliebenezet.com, you will receive a personal note of thanks from the author and answers to any questions you might have on your favorite hook. Any other comments or questions for the author on the book and leadership are welcome at the same email address.

To subscribe to our Journey of Not Knowing blog, go to
http://journeyofnotknowing.com/blog/

Continuing the Journey

Thank you for reading *The Journey*. If you would like to move from traveling the halls of Arrow to looking deeper into your own life, consider *The Journal of Not Knowing*. Whether you are leading an organization or looking to make a personal change, the journal will guide you through a mission of self-discovery.

To be used in conjunction with the *Journey* book or by itself, the workbook contains provocative questions, exercises, and other tools to explore the Journey principles of navigating the unknown, dealing with risk, and the Core Four principles.

You can explore and create a plan to address:

- Your relationship with the unknown.

- How you handle not knowing whether your ideas will turn out, including people's reactions to them (and you).

- How discomfort with uncertainty shows up in your life and gets in the way of you trying new ideas and behaviors.

- How you can get comfortable with the discomfort of the risk that comes with the unknown.

- How you can avoid sabotaging yourself with defensive behaviors.

- What purpose will give you fuel to navigate the discomfort of the unknown you might encounter on the way to pursuing your dreams.

Please visit
www.juliebenezet.com/book
for purchasing options

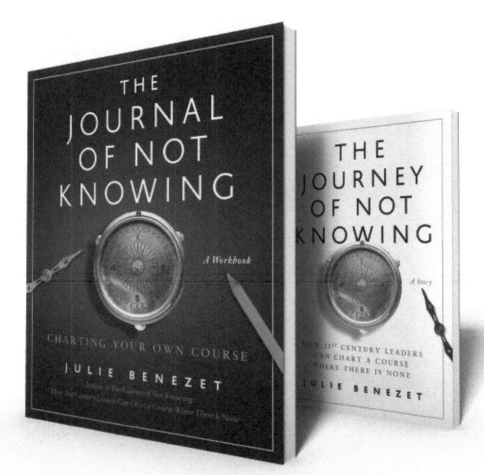

Made in USA - North Chelmsford, MA
1045670_9780997813906
01.21.2020 1543